Joseph Whitman Bailey

**The St. John River in Maine, Quebec, and New Brunswick**

Joseph Whitman Bailey

**The St. John River in Maine, Quebec, and New Brunswick**

ISBN/EAN: 9783337240745

Printed in Europe, USA, Canada, Australia, Japan

Cover: Foto ©Andreas Hilbeck / pixelio.de

More available books at **www.hansebooks.com**

THE GRAND FALLS OF THE ST. JOHN

# THE ST. JOHN RIVER

## IN MAINE, QUEBEC, AND NEW BRUNSWICK

BY

## J. W. BAILEY

CAMBRIDGE
Printed at the Riverside Press
1894

# CONTENTS.

# CONTENTS.

# THE ST. JOHN RIVER.

## CHAPTER I.

### INTRODUCTORY.

OF the many rivers of Northeastern America, it would be difficult to find one which, in the diversity of its natural features, the facilities afforded for sportsmen, and the interesting history of its colonization, is more worthy of mention than the St. John; and yet this river, viewed in its entirety, has never formed the subject of any published work. Possibly the fact that the area drained by it lies partly in the United States and partly in Canada accounts for this. The patriotic Canadian does not care to eulogize the vast wilderness of Northern Maine, which, if the assertions of provincial geographers are true, was unjustly carved out of New Brunswick by the much abused Ashburton Treaty. The American, on the other hand, is not very eager to expatiate upon the natural resources of a country that he might prefer to possess as a fractional part of his own. Be that as it may, an attempt will be made in the succeeding pages to give a comparatively full description of the St. John, with all the larger tributaries, commencing at the extreme source in Northwestern Maine, and ending at St. John city, the commercial metropolis of New Brunswick, where the river finally unites its waters with those of the Bay of Fundy.

The principal difficulty to be encountered in a work of this kind is the mass of detail, and the necessity of describing fifty or more different streams in more or less similar terms, without omitting facts that are of interest to the tourist, or stating them in the monotonous phraseology of the ordinary guide-book. Narratives of canoe voyages, stories of the camp, exploits of well-known hunters and fishermen, are but passingly touched upon, the design being rather to state, as concisely as possible, what objects of interest, opportunity for pleasurable " outings," and facilities for sport, await those who wish to visit the regions of Maine, Quebec, and New Brunswick, drained by the St. John, and its more important tributaries.

The plan adopted is to treat the river, first as a whole, and in comparison with other rivers; and then in detail, by sections, each section including some portion of the main river worthy of special notice, or a principal tributary, or group of smaller ones. Finally, there follow a few general remarks on the action of ice and floods, with other less important physical phenomena, and a brief description of the fisheries.

## COMPARISON WITH OTHER RIVERS.

As the Hudson, the Saguenay, and the St. John present more natural attractions than any other rivers of corresponding size between the Atlantic coast and the central plateau of the North American continent, a few words of comparison between them may be appropriate.

The Saguenay, from Chicoutimi to Tadousac, flows through a cañon, flanked by vast Laurentian cliffs, that rise, sometimes perpendicularly from the water's edge, to heights varying between five hundred and two thousand feet. These massive walls of rock are usually bare of all vegetation except lichens and mosses, but where the inclination permits, small spruces and firs have gained a precarious foothold. The scenery is not pretty, but decidedly impressive. A few years ago some gentlemen from Ottawa entered the Saguenay in the night, and anchored at St. Etien, a small village below Marguerite Bay. One of the party, having climbed on deck while the cliffs were bathed in the weird light of early dawn, and silently observed the surroundings, remarked, "This is gloomy, grand, and peculiar." Possibly no other sentence could so aptly describe the scene.

Forty miles from Chicoutimi the river expands

to form Lake St. John, a larger body of fresh
water than either the Hudson or St. John river
possesses. The lake is fed by the Askaapmou-
chowan, Mistassini and Peribonka rivers, all
great streams, flowing through the unexplored
wilderness of Northern Quebec. Between the
lake and Chicoutimi the descent is considerable,
affording plenty of " rapid-shooting " for ambitious canoeists.

The Hudson is the most, as the Saguenay is
the least, densely populated of the three rivers
under discussion. None of the tributaries, small
or large, are unmapped or unexplored ; and only
those rising in the Adirondacks attract the sportsman and lover of wild life. While almost as
mountainous as the lower Saguenay, the various
elevations are much less precipitous, affording
rarely beautiful sites for residences and summer
hotels. Here and there an historic fortress may
be seen, perched Rhinelike on some beetling crag,
and near the water's edge, on both sides of the
river, many tunnels and excavations have been
made in the construction of the two great railways that carry the bulk of traffic between "the
Empire City " and the West.

The St. John is less grand than the Hudson,
less impressive than the Saguenay, but excels
both in the diversity of its natural features. For
seventy-five miles, commencing at the source, it
flows through a great forest, the home of the

moose, caribou, deer, bear, and beaver. Then
scattered settlements appear, or isolated houses,
separated from all others of their kind by wide
expanses of woodland and rough water. One
hundred and ten miles from the source, these settlements begin to be connected by a continuous
road, and the valley is good for agriculture, and
peopled almost exclusively by the French. At
Grand Falls, midway between the source and
mouth, the character of the civilization changes,
the French colonists having been gradually sup-
planted by others, chiefly of English, Irish, and
Scottish origin.

The physical features alter in a manner quite
equally marked as the distance from the source
increases. Sluggish waters flowing through desolate barrens, or lowlands covered with a dense
growth of spruces and firs, are succeeded by miles
of swift current and rocky rapids. Below Allagash the stream widens, and incloses many alluvial islands of great fertility. At the Grand Falls
the water plunges over a precipice nearly eighty
feet high, and careers tumultuously through a
rocky gorge. The current is very rapid below
the falls, and remains so almost to Fredericton,
while the hills surrounding the valley are quite
high, and generally under cultivation. Between
Fredericton and Belleisle the current is sluggish,
and the river broadens and deepens, once more
inclosing a multitude of islands, all of alluvial

deposit. Lastly the country assumes a mountainous character, although the elevations cannot
compare with those of the Hudson or the Saguenay, and great parallel arms or lakes extend eastward, offering almost unrivaled facilities for inland navigation. It would be idle to say that the
St. John is more or less interesting than the Hudson, or the Hudson than the Saguenay, as opinions
vary in this regard with the peculiar tastes, or
nativity, of the persons who offer them.

Measured from the St. John Ponds at the
source of the South Branch to the Bay of Fundy,
the St. John is probably four hundred and forty-
six miles long, or a little more than one tenth the
length of the longest river in the world, the Mississippi, measured from the source of the Missouri
to the Gulf of Mexico. It is one hundred and
fifty miles longer than the Hudson, and somewhat
more than half as long as the Rhine, while the
drainage basin has been computed at twenty-six
thousand square miles, about one ninetieth that
of the Amazon.

# CHAPTER II.

## THE UPPER ST. JOHN.

### THE BAKER AND SOUTHWEST BRANCHES.

OF the two streams which form, by their union, the St. John River, one rises in a group of very small ponds distant one hundred and fifty miles from the Atlantic coast and eighty-two miles from the St. Lawrence River, the other in a small lake, named Lac St. Jean, about twenty miles farther westward. The first of these, usually called the Baker, or South Branch, is somewhat longer than the second, or Boundary Branch ; but when standing on the point at the junction of the two streams, it is difficult to determine which is the larger in volume, by reason of their close resemblance. Both lie in an absolutely unbroken wilderness, large tracts of swampy forest land and low hills being the characteristic features of the region. As might be expected, these forests abound with moose, deer, and caribou. The deer are rapidly increasing in number, and one often hears them lowing at night, and splashing about the marshes, or surprises them in the water, while paddling swiftly and noiselessly around the many bends of the stream. The moose are diminishing here, as elsewhere, and must eventually share the fate of the buffaloes on the Western prairies.

The Southwest or Boundary Branch is important as forming for some distance the International Boundary, here dividing the Province of Quebec from the State of Maine, and there is a monument on it, erected by the boundary commissioners. Sportsmen seldom visit it, there being no convenient way of reaching the upper waters except by ascending the stream. The Baker Branch, on the contrary, which rises in seven or eight small ponds (the latter forming the real sources of the St. John), may be quite easily reached by a carry of two miles from the Northeast Branch of the Penobscot. The streams flowing from these ponds unite and empty into St. John Pond, some two miles and one half long by one mile broad. Eighteen miles of canoeable stream connect St. John Pond with Baker Lake, a rather uninteresting body of water about three miles long, surrounded by low, thickly wooded hills, and often inaccurately spoken of as the source of the St. John River. Above the lake a large brook enters the Baker stream from the west, a rough and rocky brook to navigate, but one affording another portage to the Northeast Branch of the Penobscot, at Abakcotnetick Bog. For a few miles below Baker Lake the water runs over a ledge-obstructed, bowlder-strewn bed in a suc-

cession of active little rapids; then begin the
" deadwaters," [1] so characteristic of the region.

The Southwest Branch is similar to the Baker,
being rapid for several miles above the mouth,
and sluggish in its middle course. The distance
to the Bay of Fundy from the head of Baker
Lake, following the river, is four hundred and
twenty-three miles, and from the fork of the two
branches four hundred and two miles.

## THE NORTHWEST BRANCH.

The St. John is rapid at first below the forks,
and then flows placidly on to the junction of the
Northwest Branch, twelve miles below the Baker.
This branch is larger than the others, and at the
mouth is very wide and shallow, and strewn with
bowlders. Eight miles from the St. John it
forks, the principal branch being called the Daaquam, or Quam, while the smaller one retains
the name of the main stream, — a geographical
misnomer, quite as apparent, although hardly as
important, as the Mississippi-Missouri one. Canoeists may reach the Quam by road from St.
Valier, a station on the Intercolonial Railway,

[1] The writer introduces the term "deadwater," as one of
marked local significance, and apologizes in advance for a frequent use of it. When a stream becomes tortuous and deep,
with a current almost imperceptible in the summer months, and
the banks are low and covered with rank marsh grass, or
densely tangled thickets of alder bushes, the natives call it a
" deadwater."

twenty-three miles east of Quebec city. The distance is forty-six miles. Then twenty-two miles of down-stream paddling brings them to the St. John River, the first fourteen miles being on the Daaquam, where the water is "dead" (technically speaking), and the banks richly wooded. Lumbermen say that the best timber cut above Allagash comes from the various tributaries of the Northwest Branch, all of which, excepting the headwaters of a few small brooks, lie in a wilderness as yet uninvaded by other than the canoeist, hunter, and woodsman. Small trout are quite numerous in some of these waters, but the sportsman is advised to go elsewhere if fishing is his primary object.

Some years ago the Northwest Branch was the scene of a mournful tragedy. A Frenchman, traveling in the wood, stepped suddenly upon a steel trap, attached by a chain, in the usual way, to a heavy spruce log, and covered with brush and moss. His foot was caught, and vain were all attempts to loosen it. Imprisoned in a trackless forest, mocked by the echoes of his cries for help, he met a lingering death by famine and exposure. Bears are usually caught by steel traps, and they have been known to drag the heavy chains and logs for some distance, and finally gnaw their captured paws off, while struggling savagely for freedom.

## SEVEN ISLANDS AND VICINITY.

Between the Northwest Branch and Seven Islands, twenty-six miles, the river is wide, shallow, rocky, and rapid. The rapids are not bad enough to worry a veteran canoeist, but the main St. John, and in fact all tributaries above Allagash, drop so low in occasional dry seasons that it becomes almost impossible to navigate them at all. Some gentlemen from Boston — and they were veterans too, fearing nothing from the moose to the mosquito — spent eight days in wading and dragging a canoe from the St. Valier road to the Islands. At that time, however, the water was exceptionally low.

Burntland Brook, which enters the river from the north, six miles below the Northwest Branch, has a deep pool near the mouth, where, at times, trout of the first magnitude may be caught in abundance. The Northwest Rapid, also, is reputed to be a good fishing-ground.

Seven Islands, the most remote settlement on the St. John, was founded about sixty-five years ago, and named inappropriately from the presence of thirteen alluvial islands that here obstruct the channel. It now consists of half a dozen large and comfortable farms, having no means of communication with the rest of the civilized world but by the river and a rough wood road leading to St. Pamphile, a small village of Quebec sit-

uated thirty-six miles from the St. Lawrence at
L'Islet. The road traverses the most aggravating
sloughs and swamps, and travelers who reach the
Islands that way generally prefer to return by
water. As a good portage, thirteen miles in
length, connects the Currier farm at The Islands
with Harvey's Depot farm on the Allagash, the
tourist is advised to cross over and enjoy the superior sporting facilities of that stream.

### FROM THE ISLANDS TO THE ALLAGASH.

Below Seven Islands, and almost all the way to
Allagash, a distance of fifty miles, the St. John
is shallower, and even more rocky and turbulent
than it is above the Islands, and two rapids, the
most dangerous on the river, are found here.
One, called " Big Black River Rapid," where the
water falls for half a mile over ledges of slate, in
a channel plentifully bestrewn with jagged bowlders, is a mile above Big Black River, and twenty
miles below the Islands; while the other, called
the " Big Rapid," begins about three miles above
Little Black River, and forms a succession of
small cascades and frothy pools, aggregating
nearly two miles in length. Fewer ledges appear
in the " Big " than in the Big Black River Rapid,
but more bowlders obstruct the channel; both are
very dangerous for other than the experienced
native to navigate. In the spring, when the
waves are heavy, bateaux are often swamped, and

occasionally a life is lost; yet in spite of these great rapids, and many smaller ones, heavy tow boats, laden with horses, hay, and lumbermen's supplies, ascend the river, at medium water, to the Baker Branch. Heavy horses, used to wading over the roughest river bottom, supply the power, and the stream-drivers, with ropes and poles, strive diligently to keep the unwieldy craft in the proper channel.

Navigation is certainly bad, whether for canoe or bateau, between the Northwest Branch and Allagash, and the scenery is, as a rule, monotonous, and nowhere very picturesque. A few scattered settlers are found, principally around the mouths of the Little Black and Chemquassabamticook rivers, but having no means of communication with the outside world, except by the rough river, their mode of life is very primitive. One man, the solitary occupant of a frame house on the left bank, eleven miles from his next door neighbor, was, a few years ago, forgetting human speech, and finding it quite a difficult task to think of words proper for the conveyance of the most ordinary ideas. Above the Big Rapids lived a family of which no member had ever seen a railway or a telegraph wire. Some of the boys had never seen a photograph, or even an ordinary highway road. The mother had traveled as far as Edmundston, or Little Falls, which she implicitly believed to be a metropolis of colossal proportions. Certainly the education of the "Chem-quassabamticookers" has been neglected in some respects, but they have a vast knowledge of wood-craft, canoe - poling and stream - driving, all of which sciences are sadly neglected in our greater universities.

Canoe-poling really is a science. The polers gradually urge the canoe to the foot of the rapid, where the water tumbles and tosses furiously through narrow channels, separated by bowlders or ledges; and then, glancing hastily up-stream to determine which of these tortuous channels is straightest or deepest, they give a sturdy shove, and the bow of the frail craft is almost buried in the foaming waters. When the force of the first push is spent, the bow is often out of water, the stern deeply sunk in the frothy pool below. Then the bow-poler digs his pole into some crevice between the rocks, and there holds it, trembling with the mighty force of the current, until the stern man has reset his own pole a few feet up the stream, and prepared for another her-culean effort. So great is the power of the water, that a deviation of but a few inches from the direction of its flow may cause the canoe to be swung broadside upon some sharp and jagged rock. The Indians consider it more dangerous to descend some of the longer rapids than to pole up, as in places where unexpected peculiarities in the channel necessitate a sudden change of course, the canoe may have attained a momentum extremely difficult to check.

## BIG AND LITTLE BLACK RIVERS.

The Big Black River rises west of St. Pamphile in Quebec, runs about forty-five miles, and empties into the St. John twenty-one miles below Seven Islands. The headwaters of both the main stream and Depot stream, or principal western branch, interlock with the Northwest Branch of the St. John. The river lies almost totally in the wilderness, but a few tributaries traverse the clearings of St. Pamphile, and the road to Seven Islands crosses the main stream and Depot Branch. The word "depot," in sylvan dialect, means a storage camp where lumbermen resort for supplies. One of these is on the Depot Branch. The hunters choose various places for storing provisions, including the hollowed trunks of old decayed trees. On one occasion a novice and his guide were lost, and the novice expressing anxiety about the meagre food supply, the guide jocosely remarked: "I can kick bread and molasses out of most any stump."

At average water the canoeing is good below St. Pamphile, and the principal branches of Black River are also more or less navigable. The Indian name of the river is Chimpassacoutie; of its North Branch, Metawaakwamis. Very extensive deadwaters occur both on the main stream and tributaries. The fishing is poor, but game quite plentiful, — deer especially so.

The two Black Rivers have been named from the dark color of their waters; a color partly derived, it seems, from the numerous deadwaters, where the soft muddy banks are easily eroded, and much vegetable matter settles and decays. They are not the sole cause, however, as some streams are wine-colored from organic or mineral impurities above the deadwaters, and the little Oroquois River, below Edmundston, is quite half deadwater, yet very clear.

Little Black River, having the same general characteristics as Big Black, enters the St. John three miles above Allagash. A few settlers live at the mouth, above which the whole river basin is surrounded by what Thoreau calls " the grim untrodden wilderness, whose tangled labyrinth of living, fallen and decaying trees only the deer and moose, the bear and wolf can easily penetrate."

The settlers are very poor. When an explorer was about to throw away a well-picked ham bone, the guide arrested his arm, saying that he would take it to one of the houses, where the gift would be appreciated, — probably as a suitable ingredient for soup.

## LAC DE L'EST.

About midway between Big and Little Black rivers the St. John receives the Chemquassabamticook, a considerable stream flowing from Lac de L'Est. The Allagash has a tributary of the same name, the natives pronouncing it "Se-bam-se-cook."

Surrounded as it is by lofty forest-clad hills, that rise quite abruptly from the water's edge, Lac de L'Est presents more attractions than any other lake of the St. John system above the Allagash. It teems with mammoth trout, and the touladi (*salmo ferox*) is equally plentiful. July is the best month for fishing. The only settlement is the little plantation of the Indian Louis John, connected by thirteen miles of very rough wood road with the French settlements southeast of Kamouraska. The lake measures nine miles in length, and the international boundary crosses it two miles above the outlet. Natives say that the stream would be readily canoeable, at average water, from Lac de L'Est to the St. John, a distance of eighteen miles, if the channel was freed from obstructions; but a reliable explorer says: "I have seen the bed of the Chemquassabamticook perfectly dry in the latter part of August."

## DRAINAGE AREAS.

The total drainage area of the St. John, with
tributaries, above the Allagash, is 2,950 square
miles, of Big Black River, about 600 square miles,
of the Northwest Branch, about 550 square miles,
of the St. John, with tributaries, above the Northwest Branch, 770 square miles, and of Little Black
River, 310 square miles.

The Seven Islands are 365 miles, and the
mouth of the Allagash 315 miles, from the sea at
St. John city.

## THE ALLAGASH RIVER.

The Aroostook, Tobique, Jemseg, Allagash, and
Madawaska are the five tributaries of the St. John
having drainage areas over one thousand square
miles in extent. That of the Allagash is 1,450
miles, including the basins of the two principal
branches, the Chemquassabamticook and Musquacook. The river is more picturesque, and in
every way more attractive than the main St. John
above it; the waters abound with fish; the neighboring forests with moose, deer, and caribou.
Beaver are found on the small tributary brooks,
but not more frequently than on other remote
watercourses in Northern Maine and New Brunswick.

The source of the Allagash is not over ten
miles, in a straight line, from the junction of the

Southwest and Baker branches of the St. John, and the river flows easterly at first, through Allagash Lake into Chamberlain Lake. Allagash Lake may be reached by portage from Poland Brook, a stream flowing indirectly into the West Branch of the Penobscot, and is quite large, with precipitous rocky shores on the western side. Travelers say the fishing is good near the river's inlet. A courageous canoeist may ascend the Allagash for many miles above the lake and portage to Lac Yule, the head of the Chemquassabamticook; but novices are respectfully advised to refrain from any such undertaking.

From Allagash Lake to Allagash Pond, a distance of two or three miles, the current is rapid; and between the pond and Chamberlain Lake there are two falls, many rapids, and several little deadwaters. From Mud Pond, which connects with Chamberlain Lake by a small, sluggish brook, a well-known portage, two miles in length, leads to the Umbazookscus Lake and Stream, the latter waters flowing into the West Branch of the Penobscot. Many travelers from Moosehead Lake pass this way, the carry having been much improved in recent years. Thoreau, who crossed it in 1857, says: " I would not have missed that walk for a good deal. If you want an exact receipt for making such a road, take one part Mud Pond, and dilute it with equal parts of Umbazookskus and Apmoojenegamook ; then send a fam-

ily of musquash through to locate it, look after
the grades and culverts, and finish it to their
minds, and let a hurricane follow to do the fen-
cing."

The Fish, Madawaska, Jemseg, and Allagash
rivers probably have more lake surface within
their collective drainage basins, — if we exclude
the bays and fiords of the lower St. John, — than
all other tributaries combined.  Over one hundred
lakes and ponds pay tribute to the Allagash, and
of these, Chamberlain Lake is much the largest.
The famous Chamberlain farm, where supplies
may be obtained, is the only settlement to break the
monotony of its forest-clad shores.  Eagle Lake,
sixteen miles long, is next below Chamberlain,
and next in size, connecting with Churchill Lake
or Wallagasquequam, the third in the chain, by
a still-water thoroughfare.  Several brooks fall
into Eagle Lake, which is irregular in outline,
and very picturesque, inclosing a couple of large
wooded islands.  Pillsbury Island is the more
southerly of these, and, almost opposite, Smith
Brook flows in from the east, a stream " canoeable " to its source in Haymock Lake.  Russell,
Soper, and Snare are three other large brooks entering the Allagash in Eagle Lake ; all fairly good
trout streams, partially navigable for canoes.
Thoroughfare Brook above Churchill Lake is
also a considerable stream, much resembling those
last named.

Below the outlet of Chamberlain Lake, the lumbermen have, for many years, maintained a dam, by means of which, and a canal connecting Chamberlain and Telos lakes with Webster Brook, the most material part of the upper Allagash is turned down the East Branch of the Penobscot. Thus we have the rare phenomenon of one stream entering two rivers. Chamberlain Lake forms the connecting link, and, in the freshet season especially, flows both east and north, like the Cassaquiare in South America, a stream joining the Orinoco River with the Rio Negro, a branch of the Amazon.

The effect of such a dam upon lake scenery is truly startling. The sandy beaches disappear, the waves break rudely on the forest, the stately trees, beaten by drifting ice, rotted by unnatural submersion, fall prone upon the water; and their weakened, sapless trunks are piled in much confusion against the dense green wood behind, forming a tangled maze of stumps, and roots, and branches, on which the stormy waters vainly break. So does Nature seemingly resent the spoliation of her works by man.

A few rods below Churchill Lake are the ruins of another dam, which once stemmed back an immense body of water, and was erected by the Yankee lumbermen in order to drive the St. John lumber down the East Branch of the Penobscot, via Telos Lake, the New Brunswick government having levied a duty on logs cut in Maine, in alleged violation of the Treaty of 1842.[1] The dam was finally destroyed by a party of men in the employ of John Glazier, Esq., of Fredericton, and so great was the volume of water discharged that the St. John River rose three feet at Grand Falls, one hundred and sixty-five miles away.

[1] Sec. 111. Of the Treaty between the States and Great Britain, 1842. In order to promote the interests and encourage the industry of all the inhabitants of the countries watered by the River St. John's and its tributaries, whether living within the State of Maine or the Province of New Brunswick, it is agreed that where, by the provisions of the present treaty, the River St. John's is declared to be the line of boundary, the navigation of the said river shall be free and open to both parties, and shall in no way be obstructed by either; that all the produce of the forest in logs, lumber, timber, boards, staves, or shingles, or of agriculture, not being manufactured, grown on any of those parts of the State of Maine watered by the River St. John's or by its tributaries, of which fact reasonable evidence shall, if required, be produced, shall have free access into and through the said river and its tributaries, having their source within the State of Maine, to and from the seaport at the mouth of the River St. John's, and to and from the falls of the said river, either by boats, rafts, or by other conveyance; that, when within the Province of New Brunswick, the said produce shall be dealt with as if it were the produce of the said province; that, in like manner, the inhabitants of the territory of the upper St. John's, determined by this treaty to belong to her Britannic majesty, shall have free access to and through the river for their produce, in those parts where the said river runs wholly through the State of Maine: Provided, always, That this agreement shall give no right to either party to interfere with any regulations not inconsistent with the terms of the treaty, which the governments, respectively, of Maine or of New Brunswick may make respecting the navigation of said river, where both banks thereof shall belong to the same party.

For half a mile below the ruined dam there are rapids, the worst on the Allagash, but pigmies when compared with those near Black River on the St. John. In the very midst of one of them, called the "Devil's Elbow," the canoeist must cross at a right angle with the current, or be dashed on jagged rocks, upset, and wrecked. With a loaded canoe strong hands and steady nerves are required to avoid some such calamity, and the novice had better explore the portage called Chase's carry.

Churchill Lake is a delightful expanse of water, about six miles long by four broad, receiving, like Eagle Lake, the contributions of many brooks. Two of these brooks, called the "Twins," enter from the southwest, the North Twin being the outlet of Spider Lake, a dark and deep water, swarming with different fishes, and named from its very irregular shore line. A small brook struggles in at the head of Spider Lake through a rather grewsome cedar swamp, where a portage leads to the deadwater of the Munsungan, a branch of the Aroostook. Indians often passed this way in former days, and in 1887 the writer observed a rude picture of a savage chief, carrying a birch canoe, which was carved on a tree trunk, with certain signs to indicate the portage.

A lone hunter lives on Spider Lake, guarding a depot camp. His sole companion is a cat, which, for the sake of increased proficiency in keeping

troublesome rodents from the supplies, is compelled to live on what it captures *vi et armis*.
We saw it pounce upon a mouse, and swallow the
unfortunate animal, yet squeaking, with no more
attempt at mastication than a commercial traveler makes in a railway restaurant.

An interesting trip, through a picturesque, unbroken wilderness, is that from Spider Lake, via
Pleasant and Harrow lakes, to the Musquacook,
the second in length and volume of the many
tributaries of the Allagash. The portage to Pleasant Lake is a mile and a half long, and that from
Pleasant to Harrow Lake a little over a mile. All
told there are six lakes on the main Musquacook
stream, the uppermost one, Clear Lake, nestling
at the base of Round Mountain, and affording
some striking scenery. The others are connected
by navigable thoroughfares, and the old wood
road from Seven Islands to Allagash passes near
the outlet of the first lake, from which point it
is a ten-mile walk to Harvey's Depot farm on the
Allagash. Musquacook stream, below the lakes,
is usually navigable for canoes.

Long Lake, the nucleus of the Allagash system, is, like Chamberlain, Eagle, and Churchill
lakes, a mere fluvial expansion. It is ten miles
long and divided by a narrow thoroughfare into
two parts, called, respectively, Upper and Lower
Umsaskis. The Chemquassabamticook River
(already mentioned), which unites with the Up-

per Umsaskis, is navigable for canoes to Lac Yule, although, for the most part, a broad and shallow stream. Lac Yule is one of the largest lakes of the Allagash country, and was represented on early maps, when the region was little explored, as draining into the St. John River above Seven Islands. Both Upper and Lower Umsaskis are charmingly picturesque, and afford excellent opportunities for angler and hunter. One Harvey, a famous woodsman, thoroughly conversant with the geographical intricacies of the region, has a depot farm near the foot of the lower lake, where the traveler may take the portage to Currier's farm at the Seven Islands.

It is questionable if a better river for the canoeist can be found anywhere than the Allagash below Harvey's. Almost everywhere the current is swift, and ever and anon the water dashes down a sand-bar, gradually narrowing as it descends, until a myriad of dancing pyramidal shaped waves are formed by the action of cross currents and eddies. These waves have been rather oddly termed "hay-stacks." The woods are rich in game, more especially near Petaguongomis, or Round Pond, an oval-shaped fluvial expansion three miles above Musquacook.

Above the Great Fall, fourteen miles from the mouth, the water scatters into many channels, which inclose a cluster of islands very similar to the Seven Islands on the St. John; and a few pioneer settlers live in this vicinity. The fall is almost thirty feet high, and second in magnitude among all waterfalls of the St. John River system. Below, the stream is rocky, with many rapids, of which those at Two Brooks are most exciting, although not dangerous. The waters finally discharge by two channels, which inclose Gardner's Island between them.

The Allagash and St. Francis rivers are the only large tributaries of the St. John with well-formed deltas at their mouths.

### FROM ALLAGASH TO ST. FRANCIS.

The St. John, as a really large river, commences at the mouth of the Allagash, the latter stream probably having a volume of discharge two thirds as great as that of the former above their junction. During the annual spring freshet the St. John is very much the larger, there being few lakes to store flood water; but as it falls so low in the dry season, there are undoubtedly times when the Allagash becomes the greater river. At Allagash, too, we find the commencement of a civilization which increases in complexity, generally speaking, all the way to the Bay of Fundy; and at Golden's farm, four miles below, the natives enjoy no less a luxury than a carriage road.

In the twelve miles between Allagash and St. Francis some lively rapids appear, Nigger Brook, Cross Rock, Golden's and Rankin's rapids being most conspicuous; while a lofty ridge, curiously serrated along the summit, and denuded by forest fires, rises abruptly on the north, lending a very distinct enchantment to the view. All the rapids are navigable, but, as the guide says: "*Prenez garde les grandes roches.*"

The Cobobscoose or Nigger Brook (the latter name was given because a negro stream-driver once found a watery grave there; Cobobscoose is not the Algonquin word for "nigger") enters near the rapid of the same name. It rises in Cobobscoose Lake, fifteen miles south of the St. John, and is, at the mouth, a noisy torrent of very clear water, giving promise of trout in the more quiet turns above.

### THE ST. FRANCIS RIVER.

The St. Francis well merits description as a river interesting alike to all classes of sportsmen. Rising in a small lake of the same name, but twelve miles from the seacoast east of Rivière du Loup, the stream actually twists across the watershed from the St. Lawrence side. It is about seventy-five miles long and drains about seven hundred square miles.

The old Temiscouata portage (a military road) and the recently constructed Temiscouata Valley Railway cross the river five miles below St. Francis Lake, and from there down the canoeing is continuously good, excepting a few natural dams of logs and drift stuff, all in the first fifteen miles. In one place, where the stream permeates such a tangled thicket of alders that the branches and twigs have knotted in a common mass across the water, the "*prenez garde*" of our infallible guide is intermingled with the more unpardonable exclamation, " *Sacre !* "

Pohenagamook, on the western shore of Boundary Lake, a village of two or three hundred souls, — French souls, — and the first settlement below the railway crossing, is connected with St. Alexandre on the St. Lawrence by a road twenty-six miles long. The lake is nine miles long, narrow and deep. Hills uprise on all sides; the alternation of wooded slopes with patches of cultivated land and fields of charred stumps adding a variety to the landscape.

From Boundary Lake to the mouth, a distance of forty miles, the St. Francis forms the international boundary. For twenty-five miles, commencing at the lake, Maine is on the west side, and Quebec on the east; for the remainder of the distance Maine still on the west side, but New Brunswick on the east.

Receiving in Boundary Lake the waters of Smoke River, and in the deadwater below those of Sal-way-e-sip, or Wild Cat Brook, and yet lower down the addition of Dead Brook, the St. Francis becomes a much more considerable stream, and glides so rapidly around a series of sharp turns that a canoe is in danger of being slapped against the bank, or carried under overhanging brush. On a late journey both these mishaps occurred. Below the round turns come the Kelly Rapids, which are said to be two miles long, but canoes have descended in eleven minutes, during high water, however long they are. The trout-fishing is very good occasionally, both in the rapids and in the deadwater below Boundary Lake.

Blue River, the one really large tributary, enters from the east, twelve miles below Pohenagamook. It is the first clear-water stream of the St. John system that we have yet met, and has two principal branches rising near Nôtre Dame de St. Louis du Ha Ha, a village on the Temiscouata road. About forty miles of its waters would be canoeable but for numerous "jams" of driftwood and fallen trees. In the summer of 1887 the East Branch was so choked with lumber, prostrate trees, old roots, and bushes, that two explorers were obliged to abandon their canoe and outfit, walk through the woods to the forks, and descend the main stream straddled on a cedar log. On this quixotic voyage they were carried backward over a smooth rapid, sent crashing through a mass of brush which overhung the eddying pool below, stranded on a sunken root, and ultimately overturned. Their feet, always in the icy water, were scraped on sand-bars over which the unmanageable log passed with much velocity, and a lack of shelter, warmth, and food added much to their discomfort. While Blue River is a much purer stream than the St. Francis, the trout-fishing is greatly inferior, — a strange fact, considering the habit of the trout to follow the clearest water. The region is an excellent one for caribou and bears.

At the Nadeau farm, three miles below Blue River, a good portage, also of three miles, leads to Cabineau Lake.

Beau Lake is quite what the name implies, — a beautiful sheet of water, nine miles long by two broad, surrounded by hills and forests as nearly virgin as one is apt to find in these days. Below the lake the river is very peculiar, appearing like a great stream newly turned down a wooded valley, no sufficient time having elapsed for the wearing out of an ordinary river channel. First we find a pond, then a lively rapid, then another pond or lake. The water rushes laterally from Cross Lake in a rapid called the "Mill Privilege," so close to the lake as to be easily seen one third way out from shore; while the outlet is so narrow that a canoeist might well pass by, and find himself in a natural cul-de-sac at the lower end. Below the Mill Privilege come the winding ledges, with more rapids, the stream here being exactly parallel with the lower part of Cross Lake, from which it has just escaped. Then come more ponds, small and cup-shaped, then Glazier Lake, or Woolas-

A "DEADWATER" ON THE BLUE RIVER

tookpectawaagomic, five miles long and very picturesque; then rapids again to the St. John River. The greatest depth of Beau Lake is about 150 feet; of Glazier Lake, 115 feet. A peculiarly pleasant feature of St. Francis scenery is the approach of forest growth to the very water's edge; but as the scenery is enhanced thereby, so is the convenience of beaching canoes diminished.

Fall Brook, named from two waterfalls each twenty or thirty feet high, and flowing from Fall Brook Lake near the valley of Little Black River, pours in from the west, one mile below Glazier Lake. A mile or so above the Second Fall begins the famous deadwater, where the trout supply, after many years of fishing, has literally proved inexhaustible. Very few of the fish are large, but an occasional one weighs three pounds.

Few canoemen leave the St. Francis without regret, as it is, *par excellence*, a river of pretty lakes and lively rapids. The water supply of all these rivers is largely regulated by the lake extent within their respective areas. The Allagash, St. Francis, Fish, and Madawaska rivers have good water at all times, while the St. John, above Allagash, and the Aroostook, become very low in dry seasons. Green River and the Tobique usually have good water, although their lake areas are comparatively small; probably because they are more largely fed by springs than are the other tributaries.

FROM ST. FRANCIS TO FORT KENT.

Between St. Francis and Fort Kent, a distance
of eighteen miles, the St. John is generally wide
and shallow, the channel often splitting to inclose
a grassy island, fringed with bushes and stately
elm-trees. The water is rapid, or " strong " as
the natives say, and falls with extraordinary velocity and much uproar over numerous sand-bars.
On each side are broad intervales, backed by hills
of uneven contour. Many consider this the most
picturesque portion of the river. The international boundary follows the thread of the stream
for seventy-two miles, beginning at St. Francis ;
the first road on the English side begins below
St. Francis stream ; and a one-train-a-day railway
follows the valley from Edmundston. At St.
Francis, also, the character of the colonization
alters greatly, the people above being of English
descent, the people below almost exclusively of
French.

Among the French we find a very peculiar class
called " Jumpers," an unfortunate people afflicted
with an hereditary nervous malady that causes
them to do the most extraordinary things, when
influenced by unusual excitement resulting from
unexpected sensations of touch and sound. A
loud shout, a sudden blow, or a rifle-crack arouses
the latent trouble, which manifests itself for but
a brief interval, leaving its subject a victim to

remorse or shame. When some " Jumpers " were taking their luncheon, while " logging," and a by-stander shouted "Strike!" the men are said to have thrown their knives and platters about most recklessly, and at a later day one of these un-happy men is said to have jumped on a revolving saw when thus unduly influenced. In 1883, while ascending the Madawaska River, the writer was requested by his guide, a self-acknowledged " Jumper," to warn him before loudly calling to people on the bank, as otherwise he might drop his pole and overturn the canoe. The "Jump-ers" seem to have originated in one locality, which was, we believe, on the American side of the boundary line and above St. Francis.

## THE GREAT FISH RIVER.

At Fort Kent, where stands an old block-house, a monument of the " bloodless " Aroostook War, Great Fish River enters the St. John from the south. It is ninety-five miles long, measuring from the source of the West Branch, with a drainage area of nine hundred and fifty square miles, thus ranking sixth among the tributaries of the St. John.

The East Branch is a mere succession of great lakes, with thoroughfares of quick water between, so little known a half-century ago that a surveyor remarked: " We are pretty certain that they have never been explored by any agent of the State,

and all that is known respecting them is derived
from the French at Madawaska." Long Lake,
twelve miles in length by two in breadth, is the
head of the chain, and attainable by a portage of
only five miles from the St. John at Frenchville.
Curiously enough, the canoeist, by making this
short carry, can paddle down sixty-five miles of
river and lake to his starting point. Such a circuitous flow of water forms a not uncommon geographical feature of the country, a similar voyage
being possible on Madawaska water, as will be
seen hereafter. Mud, Cross, and Square lakes
are other expansions of the East Branch; Square
probably having as large a superficial area as
Long Lake, although shaped more compactly.

Limestone Point, on its western shore, affords
good camping facilities, and often a refuge from
flies. When one has undergone the torture of
continual poisonous injections, he appreciates the
relief afforded by even a temporary cessation of
attacks from those carnivorous outlaws, "*les
mouches.*"

The northwestern shore of Long Lake is under
cultivation, but Mud, Cross, and Square lakes are
completely encompassed by those evergreen forests
that seem to exercise an influence similar to that
of the sea over the habits and thoughts of men,
when once inured to life within their dusky
glades.

"What is most striking in the Maine wilderness," says Thoreau, " is the continuousness of the forest, with fewer open intervals or glades than you had imagined. Except the few burnt lands, the narrow intervals on the river, the bare tops of the mountains, and the lakes and streams, the forest is uninterrupted. It is even more grim and wild than you had anticipated, — a damp and intricate wilderness, in the spring everywhere wet and miry."

The woods are most impressive at night, when one reclines on his somewhat prickly bed of boughs and hears the wind moaning mournfully among the treetops, while a deathly stillness prevails beneath, broken only by an occasional crackling of branches, which the imagination oft attributes to the bear, the bull-moose, or the restless " Indian devil." The Indian devil is that animal which, when seen, is never believed to have been seen by anybody but the person who saw it. It varies in size, shape, and degree of ferocity.

Many brooks feed the East Branch, at the mouths of which trout were once very numerous. At present all the waters of this system are sadly overfished.

Eagle Lake, in which the branches of Fish River unite, is about fifteen miles long, and bent near the middle at a right angle. The landscape is very picturesque. The eastern arm, which receives the East Branch, is wood-surrounded; while the northern arm, where the Fish River proper emanates, is thickly settled on the western side. As a result of the great volume of water poured in during the freshets, we find a much greater space between high and low water marks than on any of the other lakes.

The West Branch of Fish River, originating in Great Fish Lake, a basin supplied by large mountain brooks that interlock with the Musquacook and Machias rivers, is longer than the East Branch, and drains about four hundred and ninety square miles. The lake is attainable by canoe, after "portaging" by a small waterfall, and it is a naturally good water for trout, remote enough to prevent overfishing. The stately moose, also, monarch of the woods of Maine, pays frequent visits there, to wallow in the shallow water, and browse upon aquatic grasses and buds of water-lilies. Portage and Nadeau are the other West Branch lakes, the former seven, the latter nine miles long. Birch and Red rivers, both navigable streams, enter Nadeau Lake, a water fringed by seemingly interminable forests. The sportsman should "try a cast" at their outlets, as well as at the mouths of rivulets. A stage road connects Portage Lake settlement with Ashland, or "No. 11," on the Aroostook, crossing the West Branch a mile below Nadeau Lake.

One of the most attractive streams in the country, from the canoeist's point of view, is Great Fish River below Eagle Lake. The volume of water is heavy, with an average depth of four feet, and the rapids almost continuous ; not dangerous rapids, nor rocky, but quick " shoots " that arouse a feeling somewhat like that of falling through air. The surrounding hills are high, and afford a pleasing landscape. Unfortunately the stream is short, and " carries " must be made around the falls and the dam above Fort Kent.

The natural Fish River Fall is about twenty feet high, and beautified by jutting ledges, that beat the falling waters till they roar with rage and seek revenge by trituration.

The Allagash and Great Fish rivers are the only large affluents of the St. John flowing wholly within the State of Maine, and Fish River is the first stream, yet considered, on which a dam may be found, other than one constructed by lumbermen to facilitate stream-driving. May the other rivers remain dam-less for numerous generations !

### FROM FORT KENT TO EDMUNDSTON.

From Fort Kent to Edmundston (nineteen miles) the St. John is a swift-flowing river, containing fewer islands and sand-bars than characterize it immediately below St. Francis. An extensive intervale and low country surround the mouth of the Meruimpticook, or Baker Brook, but the valley contracts on nearing Edmundston. Fish River Rapid, two miles from the fort, is easy and pleasant to " shoot," and the current frequently breaks over rocks lying wholly or partially beneath the surface. The once beautiful approach to Edmundston is ruined by the numerous railway cuttings. Alas! railways, wherever found, seem destructive of natural scenery, and invariably more useful than ornamental.

Edmundston, or Little Falls, a cosy village of one thousand people, and the most central starting point for the neighboring sporting grounds, is situated on both banks of the Madawaska River, near its confluence with the St. John. It has an upper and a lower town, a host of indifferent hotels, a very multitude of whiskey shops. Here the St. Francis, Temiscouata, and Canadian Pacific railways have termini; the latter road following the St. John to Woodstock, one hundred and fifteen miles away, and crossing at Upper Woodstock, Andover, and Grand Falls. Edmundston is half English, half French, and was named after Sir Edmund Head, a former governor of New Brunswick.

### THE MERUIMPTICOOK RIVER.

The Meruimpticook, or Baker Brook (drainage area one hundred and fifty square miles), pours its pellucid waters into the St. John, with considerable vehemence, at a point thirteen miles above Edmundston. Meruimpticook Lake, the source of the north and principal branch, calmly reposes in a forest wilderness extending from the depression of Cabineau Lake to that of Temiscouata. It is narrow, but very deep, and surrounded by hills which rise from the shore to heights varying between one hundred and fifty and three hundred feet. Strangely enough, sportsmen seldom visit this lake, notwithstanding its proximity to a well-settled country, and its excellent reputation as a fishing place and caribou ground. The natives call it " Jerry Lake."

Baker Lake, five miles in length, which is drained by the west branch of the Meruimpti-cook, a short stream of rapid water, is well settled at the southern end, and may be reached from the St. John River, at Caron Brook, by passing over five miles of tolerably good road. A portage of four miles — quite famous for its impassability in summer — connects the north end of Baker with the south end of Cabineau Lake; another connects Baker and Enoch Baker lakes. Enoch Baker is a beautiful sheet of water, of considerable depth, with high hills rising on the western side, imme-diately from the water's edge.

The Meruimpticook stream is about twenty-five miles long, measured from the lake of that name to the St. John River, and for the most part very rapid. Descending, we find a small fall quite near the outlet of the lake, where a dam has been built, and another, three feet high, above the west branch. Passing the west branch, we reach the Murray Fall, which may be navigated,

and the Ziae Fall, much the roughest spot on the
Meruimpticook, where a portage must be made.
A few miles above the mouth, and in the low
country, begin the deadwaters, with all their customary features. That a stream should meander
a little in sluggish places is not surprising, but
the number of serpentine turns and twists in any
given mile of one of these many deadwaters
makes the weary canoeist despair of ever reaching his journey's end. Mr. Cooney, an early geo-
grapher of New Brunswick, and one meriting
praise for the animation and originality of his
language, describes these crooked courses as the
result of " a violent collision between impetuous
freshets and strong lateral resistances ; " but his
theory is somewhat incorrect, brooks being ever
most tortuous where they permeate an easily
eroded alluvium bed, and straightest where the
currents are most impetuous.

One large eastern branch enters the Meruimpticook. Who knows but what there may be a
good-sized lake upon it? The region is almost
unexplored.

Trout are plentiful between Lake Meruimpticook and the Ziae Fall, some of them large and
gamey. Altogether the river offers numerous attractions to the various classes of sportsmen.

### THE MADAWASKA RIVER.

Although the Madawaska River is one hundred
and ten miles long, when measured up the Squatook, the source is only thirty miles in a direct
line from the mouth. In drainage area (eleven
hundred and forty square miles) it ranks fifth
among the St. John's tributaries, and it flows
from many sources, the Squatook being the longest branch, the Touladi the greatest in volume of
discharge. The Squatook first runs due south,
and then almost north, turning at a very acute
angle. Beardsley Brook, which creeps lazily over
a sandy bed overhung by projections and cano-
pied by deflectant alders, enters near this angle,
and forms a part of the well-known portage leading to the main Madawaska at a point fifteen
miles from Edmundston. Here, as on Fish River,
we may make a short carry and have a down-
stream paddle of seventy-five miles to our starting
point; to add to which inducement the Squatook
is a surpassingly attractive stream, having pure,
clear water (teeming with fish), exciting rapids,
and beautiful lakes. Big Squatook Lake is nine
miles long, with a few small but high and rocky
islands dotting the surface; and from there to
Sugar Loaf Lake (eleven miles) the water is almost continuously rapid, flowing over a narrow
bed often arched by boughs. Squatook " Fall,"
so called, is a mere navigable rapid, but a canoeist

must be on the *qui vive* when descending it.   Not
far below, a natural driftwood dam necessitates a
short portage.

Sugar Loaf Lake, the third in the Squatook
chain, is named after Sugar Loaf Mountain, an
isolated peak of very curious contour near the
eastern shore.   Near its centre, directly opposite
the mountain, appears an elevated island, famous
as a camping ground, where the most picturesque
views can be obtained.   Many trout are captured
annually off the mouths of rivulets entering
Sugar Loaf Lake, while other excellent fishing
grounds, in season, are at the head of Big Squatook Lake, and in the rapids above Squatook
Fall.   The Allagash is better for large game, but
the Squatook, like Blue River, has an unenviable
reputation for bears.

Bruin is not aggressive in his ordinary moods,
but quite capable of attack when fairly brought
to bay.   It was on the Clearwater River that
some explorers met a large she-bear with cubs, at
a place where a circuitous rocky gorge cut off the
beast's retreat.   The bear charged ferociously;
but a labyrinth of fallen trees and shrubbery considerably impeding her progress, the explorers
were enabled to escape.   The imperturbability of
the guide on that occasion deserves notice.   He
looked incredulous at first, as if wondering at the
animal's audacity in attacking so old and tried a
hunter, and then remarked reproachfully, " Well,

seein' as this is the first time we 've met, you
makes yourself durn familiar."

Twenty-five miles below Beardsley Brook portage the Squatook and Touladi rivers unite, and
half a mile above this fork the Eagle and Horton
branches unite to form the Touladi. How curiously some rivers bunch together! The Nictaux
or Forks of the Tobique afford a yet more striking
illustration of the same phenomenon.

The branches present a marked contrast. The
Horton Branch is very clear and rapid, the Eagle
Branch very dark and sluggish. In the deep pool
where they meet, a fish, distinctly seen when
swimming in the Horton water, disappears from
view at once on entering the Eagle Branch. The
Horton Branch and Green River have interlocking sources; but it would be exceedingly difficult,
perhaps impossible, to carry a canoe across the
common watershed, and the former stream falls so
quickly after a rain that the canoeist wishing to
ascend must choose his time rather carefully. It
widens at one part to form Lac des Outres, below
which there is a gorge containing one fall from
six to ten feet high, with small cascades below,
a portage of half a mile leading from the fall to
the deadwater below the lake. The Big Jam,
a stupendous obstruction, famous throughout the
country, is one mile from the mouth. An extreme
crookedness in the channel, with a comparatively
straight course above, probably fostered its for-

mation by allowing large quantities of driftwood
and logs to accumulate freely; but, however that
may be, the Jam is now a mile long, and ever
increasing. It is full of holes, through which is
seen the gurgling stream beneath, and swarms
with trout. Unfortunately the angler is apt to
lose his tackle in the complex fabric of logs, roots,
and branches on trying to fish there. The lumbermen have excavated a flood channel for running logs around.

The Horton Branch is the first in a belt of
clear-water rivers that extends, we believe, to the
eastern extremity of Gaspé Peninsula, and in-
cludes such famous streams as the Restigouche,
Tobique, and Nepisiguit, with the larger tributaries of the Miramichi. It is a good trout stream,
although deep pools are scarce.

The Eagle Branch, flowing from Lac des Islets,
near the upper waters of the Trois Pistoles River,
is tortuous, narrow, and deep, arched by interlocking branches, and kissed by dangling bushes.
The current flows swiftly, eddying around the rich
alluvial banks unbroken by a single rapid. Eagle
Lake, eight miles above the Touladi forks, is
shallow, with low, flat shores, where rushes and
water-lilies grow profusely, and extend far out
into the water. A point on the southern shore,
opposite the inlet, was a favorite camping-place
with the Indians, when accustomed to pass by this
route to the St. Lawrence. Lac des Islets, a

shallow water, named from the number of small islands formed by bowlders and angular blocks of hard sandstone, may be reached by two portages from the St. Lawrence side of the watershed. The outlet, called "Rivière St. Jean," is small, and for some distance below the lake very tortuous, and overhung by alders and leaning bushes. Then the stream spreads, becoming shallow. Numerous "drift jams" occur; and a mile and a half from Lac des Aigles there is a fall of about six feet, with rough rapids above, extending half a mile. The water flows peaceably between the fall and lake.

Touladi River proper is sluggish and very deep for eight miles below the forks, and then it expands to form the Second and First Touladi lakes, both shallow and uninteresting. Rapids begin below the first lake, and culminate in the Touladi Fall, a rough descent over transverse ledges, where the unwary canoeist sometimes finds himself *in gurgite vasto*, together with his camp supplies. Such was the experience of two Fredericton college students a few years ago. The great pool below the fall, and the water-worn depressions in the ledges above, are excellent places for trout-fishing in July, and the angler may capture a five-pound fish there, if the fates are propitious. Later in the season the big trout repair to the Madawaska River, where the sluggish current and soft grassy bottom afford an exceptionally good spawning ground. The Touladi River finally discharges into Temiscouata Lake, after draining five hundred and sixty square miles, and it is the largest river in the St. John system having no settlement above its outlet.

Temiscouata (winding water) is the deepest lake in any way connected with the St. John, and fully nine times as deep as Grand Lake on the Jemseg, its only rival in superficial area. It is twenty-eight miles long by two in average width. The bottom is almost level at a mean depth of about two hundred feet, throughout the lower and central portions, the water deepening very quickly on leaving the shore. The northern arm is shallower. It is a noticeable fact that Temiscouata Lake, as well as the Madawaska and Ashberish rivers, lie in an almost direct line with the famous Saguenay gorge, but fifty miles distant.

Trout and touladi of all sizes abound in Temiscouata, and are commonly captured with trolling hooks. The mouth of Mill Brook, four miles from Détour du Lac, is probably the best place for fly-fishing.

Numerous settlements skirt the western side; on the east we find a few isolated houses unconnected with any road. Nôtre Dame de Détour du Lac, a French village charmingly situated on the hill slope midway down the lake, is, like Edmundston, a rendezvous for sportsmen. The Temiscouata Railway follows the shore for fifteen miles, disfiguring the otherwise beautiful scenery with myriads of embankments and rock-cuttings. The "Chemin Temiscouata," an old military road, by which the distance to Rivière du Loup is forty miles, strikes away from the lake above Cabineau, and near Fort Ingalls, a collection of very ruinous barracks and guard-houses. Immediately opposite, Big Mountain uprears its shaggy wooded crest, and tradition says that soldiers of the garrison sometimes swam across the intervening water to alleviate the *ennui* of frontier life.

Cabineau River is forty-one miles long from the southern end of Cabineau Lake, and drains an area of one hundred and ten square miles. The lake, which occupies the depression between Meruimpticook and St. Francis, a famous region for caribou-hunting, is thirteen miles long, with a width of one mile and less, very irregular in shape, and dotted with islands. No other lake in the vicinity has water so pure and transparent, though we have here a group of clear waters, including the Baker Brook and Blue River. Cabineau River flows through a marshy swale for six miles below the lake, where innumerable sharply pointed cedar sprigs extend over the water, and it is easily navigable for canoes, excepting a fall about twenty feet high, six miles from Temiscouata. Above the fall there are extensive deadwaters, where, five years ago, six or seven natural driftwood dams had formed. The lumbermen cleared

these dams away, together with numerous beaver
works.  The Cabineau trout are small, but the
valley affords an excellent hunting ground for
deer and caribou.

The fallow deer, common as they are to-day,
were never seen in New Brunswick before the
year 1818, at which date also wolves first appeared.  As the deer rapidly increased in numbers the wolves thrived admirably, never hesitat-
ing to devour some domestic animal when weary
of a venison diet.  While visiting Eel River Lake
in 1842, Dr. Gesner observed the remains of
three deer and a caribou that had been dragged
upon the ice and devoured, a pack of eleven
wolves crossing the lake during his visit.  "The
howlings of these anmials around my camp at
night," he says, "were truly terrific."  When in
subsequent years the number of deer diminished,
the wolves gradually disappeared as well, finally
becoming extinct; and, now that the deer are
rapidly increasing once more, an occasional wolf-
howl again breaks the sylvan quietude.  It is a
most remarkable synchronism, best accounted for
on the hypothesis that the wolves north of the
St. Lawrence, when famished, cross the ice for
plunder.

The Ashberish River, by which the Indians
formerly crossed from Madawaska to the Trois
Pistoles, enters the northern end of Temiscouata.
It has a picturesque fall six miles above the

mouth, and from there down is very tortuous and deep, although quite rapid in places.

The Madawaska River proper, twenty - two miles long when measured from Temiscouata Lake to Edmundston, has almost everywhere an even width and depth, a peaceful current, and a grassy bottom. Its valley is thickly settled, the natives spearing the large trout by the barrelful when they descend the river to spawn in August. For two miles below the lake, people say the Madawaska never freezes in the coldest weather, the village at Pole River being named *Dégelé* after this circumstance. Such a condition might be caused by the deeper Temiscouata waters circulating upwards by the suction of the river, and then taking some time to cool after exposure to the air. The old Canada line crosses the valley twelve miles from Edmundston, and here the Bossers live, mighty polers, and foremost among Squatook guides. Trout River is a considerable stream of clear water, entering from the west. Near the mouth the customary placidity of the Madawaska is broken by a few rapids, the Little Falls, from which the town of Edmundston derived its ancient name, being much the roughest. A dam has been constructed above with materials ruthlessly torn from an old stone fort on the hillside. Canoes descend the Little Falls occasionally, although the " shoot " is rather too lively for most people who travel this way.

### FROM EDMUNDSTON TO GRAND FALLS.

Below Edmundston the physical features of the
St. John change perceptibly. Although for five
miles, or down to St. Basil, the river incloses
islands, and spreads on bars, the channel soon contracts, becoming deeper and more sluggish. The
glacial action which created the Grand Falls has
in fact stemmed the water for twelve miles, or as
far as Vanburen Village, on the American bank,
the depth varying from fifteen to thirty feet, a
greater average than is found elsewhere above
Fredericton. Green and Quisibis rivers work out
through extensive clay beds, in which fossil trees
have been found. The valley, generally speaking,
is fertile. The merry Frenchman seldom over-
works to earn his daily pork and vegetables, yet
the soft notes of his violin, wafted by an evening
breeze, and the distant tread of dancers, are sooth-
ing to the weary canoeman, if not conducive to the
material prosperity of Madawaska County.

Some of these festivities (among the lower
classes) are extremely hilarious, lasting uninterruptedly for two nights and a day. The male
French often dance with clay pipes in their
mouths, and both arms around the female. It is
usually considered bad taste for any one dancer to
monopolize the floor, and the offender is occasionally ejected from the ball-room, his exit accelera-
ted by a vigorous application of pedal extremities

on the part of jealous ones unable to dance as well. This is termed " socking the boots."

Little River, a stream with many branches, enters the St. John at the very brink of Grand Falls, pouring at low water into a funnel-shaped hole or passageway, and spouting forth into the principal fall half way down the cliff.

## THE OROQUOIS RIVER.

Two miles below Edmundston the little Oroquois River unites with the St. John, a stream flowing parallel with the Madawaska, and never far distant therefrom. It is easy to navigate as far as the fall, fifteen miles from the mouth, and probably above the fall for some distance. On it we find much deadwater, very pure and transparent, however, and swarming with small trout. Large fish are seldom or never caught there. The fall is about twelve feet high, and operates a mill, which is connected by road with the Madawaska River.

## GREEN RIVER.

No tributary of the St. John rivals Green River in general attractiveness, unless perhaps the Tobique. The popular impression that it is one long, tumultuous rapid from source to mouth is untrue ; for in one place at least, above the old Albert farm, the current runs most innocently for more than a mile. Considered as a whole, Green River is undoubtedly more rapid than any other tributary, and one poler a barely sufficient motive-power for a canoe, unless the day's journey be made short. Some of the rapids are straight, others are on bends of the stream called " round turns." The most expeditious way of ascending is by fastening two canoes side by side, but somewhat apart, with poles, and procuring a strong, sure-footed horse to drag by a tow-line.

Although the drainage area is less than five hundred square miles, and the length but seventy-five miles, a sufficiency of water for canoeing may be found at all times, partly because the channel is narrow, and partly because the valley contains an astonishing number of rivulets that never dry up in summer.

About twenty miles from the source the fourth branch, or Pimouet, enters from the east, — a stream connected by a difficult portage of seven miles with the Quatawamkedgwick, the principal water of the Restigouche.

In the twenty miles between the fourth and second branches Green River is swift and shallow, with occasional good pools above ledges, in which the trout are exceptionally lively, and very beautiful in shape and markings. Here is the best fishing, and huge trout may be seen swimming in and out among the sunken roots far down in the transparent water. Green River excels all other St. John waters for trout, although the mammoth " five-pounder " is not as common as in the few great lakes, like Temiscouata; and it is the only tributary leased by the Provincial government for trout-fishing alone. At the Black Fall, one mile above the second fork, where the water tumbles down a natural sluiceway, necessitating a carry, a short portage leads to the first Green River lake.

There are, all told, six lakes upon the second fork, or Lake Branch, which drains a valley parallel with the upper Squatook. The first is nearly surrounded by hills, long, narrow, and shallow, and the water has a fall of eight feet a little below its outlet. Between the first and second lakes the stream flows principally through a spruce and cedar swamp, and is without bad rapids, if we except a small fall three quarters of the way up. Second or Mud Lake, which is nearly a mile and a half long, is bounded westerly by a lofty ridge, while on the east the water is shallow, muddy, and swampy. The third and fourth lakes are larger and deeper, and surrounded by rising ground. The fifth and sixth lakes, five miles beyond, lie close together; the former being very shallow, with a soft bottom of white mud, which the men call "paint," from its quality of sticking to the canoe poles, like white lead. High hills are seen to the northwestward, from the tops of which the guides say they can overlook Squatook Lake. Below the third lake there are three small waterfalls, each three or four feet high.

The first fork, or east branch of Green River, which has one large fall, so the guides say, enters about twenty-five miles from the mouth, and no settlements are found above it, either on main stream or tributary. For that matter, a forest almost primeval extends northward to the St. Lawrence valley, and eastward to the lower Restigouche, affording ample facilities for the enjoyment of Nature in her most unadulterated form.

The Albert farm, easily attained by a portage of nine miles from St. Basil village on the St. John, is situated in one of the most picturesque of valleys, but the Albert family, unfortunately, once the most experienced Green River guides, are situated in the Western States. Within the thirteen miles below the farm the valley is well settled, and excellent views of Green River Mountain, an obtuse peak, beautifully forest-clad, may be obtained from the water. We find heavy waterfalls five miles above the farm, and one and one half miles from the St. John River, where small milling operations are carried on.

Along the middle portion of Green River high hills inclose the valley, and, by lifting their verdant tree-clad slopes abruptly from the water, afford most attractive scenery. Natives and travelers familiar with the stream assert that the water is colored by a natural green pigment; but the writer strongly suspects that the green pigment of Green River, the blue pigment of Blue River, and the no pigment at all of the Tobique are varieties of the same thing, namely a lively imagination aroused by certain delusive optical phenomena. That the water is deliciously clear and cool everybody must agree.

## QUISIBIS RIVER.

The Quisibis River rises in two streams, which unite thirteen miles from the St. John, and have their sources near the valley of the junction stream, a tributary of Green River's eastern branch; drains one hundred and twenty square miles; and may be canoed with ease below the forks, where it is largely deadwater. Its upper valley is said to be the coldest place in the country; but if it is so, the reason is decidedly obscure. The branches are practically " uncanoeable," and each has a fall, so the natives say.

## GRAND RIVER.

Grand River, a swift and shallow stream, but one easily navigable by canoe to the Waagan Brook, eighteen miles from the mouth, enters the St. John from the east, thirteen miles above Grand Falls, and drains about one hundred and thirty square miles. A light birch might be poled much beyond the Waagan, should a sufficient reason for so doing be found. The water is comparatively impure, the fishing bad, and the stream

unimportant, except for the fact that the Waagan
and Waagansis Brooks, often called the Restigouche and Grand River Waagans, afford a ready
means of reaching the upper waters of the Restigouche. The "carry" over this watershed, and
the "carries" between the Umbazookscus and
Mud Pond on the Allagash, and between the
Nictaux and Nepisiguit lakes, are the three most
famous modern portages connecting with the St.
John or its tributaries.

## THE GRAND FALLS.

Every traveler should visit the Grand Falls.
As the water in its mad career, although ever
the same in a general way, momentarily changes
as regards the minor movements, and as the chief
beauty of the scene depends upon that constant
change, no photograph can represent nor pen describe it. The main fall is almost perpendicular,
and wider at the top than at the base. The principal part of the river flows in a black and oily-
looking mass through a depression near the centre,
and immediately beneath a huge fragment appears, called the Split Rock, upon which the waters thunder unceasingly, and rebound with more
than doubled fury. A column of spray ever rises
from this part of the fall, completely obscuring the
Split Rock at moderately high water ; and when
the sun's rays fall upon it, a gorgeous rainbow
floats in mid-air, waving its many colors over the

sombre rocks and foaming eddies. Distinct lunar rainbows are often seen. It is not so much the splendor, the speed and energy of the Grand Falls that impress one, as it is the incessancy of the display. For how many ages, we wonder, prior to man's advent on earth, did this vast torrent of tumultuous water thunder down the cliff?

On the right-hand side the stream comes over the brink in a curtain, which, at average water, is about a foot in thickness; and on the extreme right it falls into a crevice at the base of a jutting crag, the latter facing the fall. The water is collected in this crevice and thrown sideways, other waters falling on top; and when a lot of spruce logs, passing down the side pitch, runs foul of another lot coming straight over, the spectacle is inspiring.

On the left a man may climb down to the water's edge, and there obtain, if not too badly spray-drenched, a splendid view of the Split Rock. In seasons of extreme drought the river is said to contract until the flow is almost entirely within the depression above this rock, already referred to.

A winding gorge about one mile long, the sides of which are generally perpendicular, and from eighty to one hundred and fifty feet in height, has been formed by the erosive action and recession of the fall. The rocks are calcareous slates of the Upper Silurian age, with strata so curiously twisted and irregularly worn that one may climb everywhere with a firm, safe foothold. Immediately below the fall the gorge is quite wide, that is, as wide as the fall, but it narrows gradually to a point where a suspension bridge crosses, then widens again, and finally becomes narrower than ever at the lower end, and continues all the while to deepen as the distance from the fall increases. In several places steep ravines afford access to the bottom, where there are rapids of such a wild order that any attempt at navigation would prove fatal, and opposite Pulpit Rock a stairway has been constructed. The cliffs are everywhere crowned by a thick growth of young spruce-trees.

Pulpit Rock is a colossal mass overhanging the abyss, where the St. John is narrower than it is anywhere else between the confluence of the Baker and Southwest branches and the Bay of Fundy. The exact width cannot easily be measured, for the rapid below is the wildest in the gorge. The whole river seems to throw itself in one seething and spouting mass over some hidden obstruction, which is probably a many-ton mass of rock that has fallen away from the cliff, thereby creating Pulpit Rock as we now see it. A rocky promontory, perforated with water-worn wells, extends from the stairway to the rapid. "The Great Well" is about thirty feet deep, with a diameter of sixteen feet at the top, widening at the bottom. Many others are scattered over the rocks, some large, some small, and nearly all on this promon-

tory. As it is only during very high floods that
the water covers them, they must have been formed
in the post-glacial epoch, when the gorge was in
process of erosion.

Some distance below the wells, on the same side
of the stream, a great cliff overhangs, so that when
standing on the brow the water is hardly discern-
ible at the base. Here the stream is nearly as
narrow as it is beneath the Pulpit, and perfectly
still under ordinary conditions, although dark and
threatening in appearance. Above the cliff we
find the "Coffee Mill," a whirlpool deriving its
name from an extravagant propensity to spin logs
around until they are ground to a point at each
end, and generally rendered unfit for any industrial purpose.

When the annual flood is at the maximum level,
the falls present an appearance exceedingly grand
and impressive. Standing at the water's edge in
the summer season, one sees the flood lines thirty
or forty feet above, and clearly marked by the absence of all vegetation below their level. During
the famous freshet of May, 1887, the main fall was
said to be for some days simply an enormous
rapid, while at the outlet of the gorge, ordinarily
quiet, the pent-up waters burst forth with the
wildest fury. Once some heavy logs became fastened on the Split Rock; and so many others followed before the first were dislodged, that finally
both the fall and the pool below were covered, so

that men could walk anywhere over the dam with safety. After all human efforts to loosen the mass had failed, this vast accumulation of valuable timber was dislodged by a sudden rise in the water. At the Aroostook Fall, hereinafter described, a similar "jam" took place. It is no uncommon thing to see heavy logs, thirty or forty feet in length, tossed completely out of water in the rapids of the gorge, while others are sucked into whirlpools formed above projecting ledges, and spun round for many days without remission.

The St. John River is almost equally divided by the Grand Falls, they being two hundred and eighteen miles from the source of the Baker Branch and two hundred and twenty-two from the Bay of Fundy. Excepting Niagara, and a possible waterfall or two in the Labrador peninsula, these falls of the St. John are the greatest to be found east of the Mississippi valley, and fully one third the total drainage area of the river is above them. A flock of geese is said to have come over with impunity; and the story of eighty stalwart Indian braves, led to their destruction by the squaw of a hostile tribe, forms a part of the legendary history of the place. The difference in level between the upper and lower basins is one hundred and seventeen feet.

## COLEBROOKE.

Colebrooke, or Grand Falls Village, which has about one thousand inhabitants, was ambitiously laid out in wide, regular streets; but as the growth stopped shortly afterwards, the streets became quite as much frequented by pigs as by animals of the human kind. In the vicinity of the gorge great patches of turf have been uprooted by the snouts of those uncomely quadrupeds. A portage road, less than a mile long, leads around the gorge and fall, and descends very precipitously into the lower basin, where a perfectly level tract of grassy land borders the river on the west, overflowed by many springs of icy water that ooze from the base of the cliffs. Mosquitoes are found here as late as September (a gaunt and haggard brood, and venomous), while the neighboring country is said to yield two strawberry crops in one year. What magical influence over nature does the big cataract possess?

# CHAPTER III.

## THE MIDDLE ST. JOHN.

### FROM GRAND FALLS TO ANDOVER.

AT the basin below Grand Falls the river pauses, as if for needed rest, and then races away to Andover, twenty-four miles off, at an average speed of six miles an hour. Here and there some ledges cross the channel, or loose rocks obstruct the current, forming the White Rapid, Rapide de Femme, and Black Rapid, within the first four miles from Colebrooke; Frayall's Rapid, near Little River; and the Tobique Rips, opposite Indian Point. These rapids are not dangerous, and the uniform rapidity of the current makes them less noticeable than would otherwise be the case. The valley is narrow and deep, with many well-formed terraces rising one above another, and marking former water-levels of geological antiquity. An excellent field is presented for the study of glacial and post-glacial phenomena, and of surface geology, as in addition to the numerous terraces may be seen the drift-filled pre-glacial channels of the St. John around the Grand Falls, of the Aroostook around the Aroostook Fall, and of the Tobique around The Narrows.

Between Grand Falls and Aroostook the country is more rugged, and the inhabitants fewer in number than elsewhere between St. Francis and the sea, while the railway generally follows the level table-lands on the natural terraces. On the Rapide de Femme Brook, two and a half miles from Colebrooke station, the government maintains a salmon-hatchery, above which the water falls fifty feet in a series of minute cascades.

Little River, which enters the St. John three miles above Aroostook, is in itself of no importance, but it reminds one of the blundering bad taste of the early colonists in calling a dozen or more streams in western New Brunswick by that commonplace name, while so many euphonious Indian words were negligently abandoned and lost.

### SALMON RIVER.

Salmon River rises near the source of Grand River, runs a course of forty miles, drains something over two hundred square miles, and disembogues into the St. John six miles below the Grand Falls. Through a deep valley, encompassed by lofty hills clad in a dense spruce forest, the tributary stream rushes forth with a speed rarely found in such a small body of water. Crossing a rich intervale where stately elms are grouped with other trees in the regularity of an artificial park, the water of the Salmon River — and very pure, transparent water, too — dances

and sparkles, and seems momentarily to increase
in speed; while such is the force of the stream
that, in the course of time, masses of pebbles and
sand have been pushed out, crowding the main
St. John into a comparatively narrow and very
rapid channel.   One of the ablest canoe-polers of
the Madawaska valley said that he had never un-
dertaken a more difficult task than that of push-
ing a birch up the first five miles of this mad
stream.  " Worse than Green River! " he remarked, wiping the perspiration from his brow.
Salmon River may be ascended for thirty miles
or more, but nothing will be gained by so doing,
unless the explorer desires to penetrate the wilderness in a new direction.   The water is less
rapid above Foley Brook.

Salmon never resort to this river now, as once
they did, and the trout-fishing is poor.

### THE AROOSTOOK RIVER.

Six miles above Andover the Aroostook sweeps
into the St. John by a graceful bend around the
base of a lofty ridge, which terminates in a knife-
like point at the very confluence of the two waters ; and, in length one hundred and thirty-eight
miles when measured from the source of the
Munsungan, and drainage area two thousand one
hundred and sixty square miles, it is certainly the
largest tributary.  Probably the average volume
of discharge is also the greatest, but on no other

large branch of the St. John does the water fall
so low in dry weather. Even Green River, with
an area less than one fourth as great, is generally
navigable when it would be almost impossible to
work a canoe over the partially dry bed of the
Aroostook. The causes are, probably, the paucity
of large lakes which retain the flood water, the
extensive denudation of forest, and the widening
of the channel by heavy lumber driven from the
upper waters. Once the valley was famous for
white pine, but the larger trees have been pretty
well culled out in recent years. So rich and well-
irrigated is the soil that the region has been called
" The Garden of Maine."

The Munsungan stream, undoubtedly the principal branch of the Aroostook, rises near the
sources of the Musquacook River and Spider
Brook, tributaries of the Allagash, and, by uniting
with the Milnikak, Millnokett, or south branch,
forms the Aroostook proper. Both the Munsungan and Millnokett have lakes and deadwaters.
Thirteen miles of stream connect Big Munsungan
Lake with the Millnokett, and one fall occurs,
necessitating a portage for canoes. Above the
lake are deadwaters, fed by small brooks, many
of which flow from very picturesque little ponds
among the mountains.

The Millnokett stream may be reached by portaging from the East Branch of the Penobscot to
a small pond above Big Millnokett Lake. Below

the lake the channel widens into another pond, followed by a few miles of rough water, and the lower course is also somewhat obstructed by rapids. Deadwaters are found above and below the mouth of the principal tributary, the Milmigasset, a rough brook flowing from Milmigasset Lake, one of the prettiest little bodies of water in the Aroostook valley.

The Mooseluc River runs about thirty miles, drains nearly one hundred and fifty square miles, and enters the Aroostook from the north, ten miles below Millnokett. Its various sources interlock with the Munsungan, Musquacook, and Big Machias rivers; and the country comprising the valleys of these streams is one of the best, possibly the very best, of moose grounds in the St. John River basin, and a locality equally as good for deer and caribou. The traveler must be content with the hunt, however, as the fishing is very inferior. Chandler Brook joins the Mooseluc a few miles above the mouth, and drains a fair-sized lake.

A little above Umcoleus stream, and ninety-five miles by water from the St. John, begins that pioneer settlement called the Ox-bow Plantation; then the Aroostook ceases to be a wilderness river. The banks are generally under cultivation, although wooded in places; and the water glides noiselessly along, unbroken by a single rapid that the ordinary canoeist would call a bad one. The scenery is attractive, although strictly rural. The Umcoleus stream, which takes its name, as the Indians say, from a species of wild duck, may be ascended by canoe, if the poler's arm be stronger than the rapids; and at its head are deadwaters connected by a portage with a tributary of the East Branch of the Penobscot. The La Pampeag River, which is said to have been in early times the principal avenue to the Aroostook from the Penobscot country, flows between low banks incumbered with alders and leaning bushes.

The Masardis, or St. Croix River, probably the largest tributary, but one uninteresting to sportsmen, as flowing through a partially inhabited country, enters from the south, twelve miles above Ashland, and drains two hundred and sixty square miles. Big Machias River, on the contrary, another tributary draining over two hundred square miles of forest and desolate, barren land between the valleys of the Mooseluc and Fish rivers, affords an excellent hunting ground for moose and other large game.

Pending the settlement of the boundary question between the United States and Great Britain, the Aroostook valley became the prey of lawless trespassers, who removed large quantities of the most valuable timber. The legislature of Maine, in secret session, passed a resolve for the protection of the public lands, and authorized Sheriff

Strickland to muster a company of volunteers for
the suppression of this illegal traffic. On the
fifth day of February, 1839, two hundred men
were marching through the wilderness, under the
leadership of Captain Stover Rines, and on the
eighth of that month they reached Masardis
stream, fell unexpectedly upon the trespassers,
who offered but slight resistance, and captured
their teams and implements. Flushed with success the company then advanced to the Little
Madawaska, where they met with a reverse, and
Captain Rines was made a prisoner, and carried
off to Fredericton. These events precipitated the
so-called "Aroostook War," a general call to
arms throughout the Provinces and Maine, for-
tunately unattended with loss of life, and leading
to some curious international complications and
Lord Ashburton's treaty.

Ashland village, forty-five miles by road from
the St. John River, is prettily situated on a hill-
top overlooking the great green forest of the
Machias valley. It is the terminus of a lumbermen's road that extends almost straight across
northern Maine to the Quebec settlements, crossing the Musquacook and Allagash rivers, and
connecting Seven Islands with St. Pamphile.
Few but Indians can trace it now, so overgrown
has it become in many places with young trees
and dwarfish shrubbery.

Midway between Masardis and Machias the

Aroostook receives the Squapan, a "canoeable" stream, issuing from a lake nine miles in length, the largest in the Aroostook valley.

From Ashland to Presque Isle the river is shallow and very broad, — in places as broad as the main St. John above Edmundston. The town of Presque Isle, a miniature metropolis of four thousand people, built across the Presque Isle stream, one mile above its confluence with the Aroostook, has sprung mushroom-like, in a few years, from two houses and a mill; while the villages of Caribou and Fort Fairfield, the former fourteen, the latter twenty-six miles below Presque Isle, have also had a rapid, prosperous growth. Presque Isle stream resembles the Masardis; and as the upper waters interlock with those of another Presque Isle, a tributary of the St. John, the two streams are called respectively the Aroostook and St. John Presque Isles by way of distinction. Although but sixteen miles from Presque Isle town to the St. John, the distance is thirty-three miles by the river, which makes a very sharp northward bend. Below Caribou the Little Madawaska enters the Aroostook from the north, a large stream draining two hundred and thirty square miles south of the east branch of Fish River, and said to be sluggish, flowing through swampy forests of spruce and fir.

Four miles from the mouth, the noble Aroostook sadly impairs its reputation as a stream of uninterrupted tranquillity. The water divides at first into little rapid channels, which gradually contract and unite; the slope of the river bed and the force of the current ever increasing, until the river finally enters a gorge, and tumbles about in it with a wanton fury only exceeded by that of the St. John at the Grand Falls. The walls of the gorge are low at first, but rise to an elevation of sixty or seventy feet at the lower end. Within are five principal cascades aggregating seventy-five feet in height; the largest a fall of sixteen feet, at the foot of the gorge, where a remarkable dike of diorite overhangs the water. Immediately below the dike is the Split Rock, on which lumber once piled, as at the Grand Falls, until the gorge became completely choked. Nicely formed wells appear at the Aroostook Falls, worn out by the grinding action of rounded stones, and one especially is very large, the water within pulsating in correspondence with the ebb and flow of the fall outside, by reason of some curious subterranean connection. Dense evergreen woods surround the gorge, and the scene is picturesque in the extreme.

The valley of the Aroostook, in the three miles intervening between the fall and mouth, is very deep, and in several places the water falls over ledges and bowlders, forming rough rapids. Whatson's and Herd's rapids are the most dangerous to navigate, and are already responsible for one or two canoe wrecks and some loss of life. In 1842 a canoe containing Dr. Gesner and his Indians was carried over Whatson's Rapid and swamped, much to the doctor's vexation, as he had intended to confine his geological researches to such ledges as appeared above water. The Augeanquapsporhegan, or Limestone River, enters from the north near Herd's Rapid by successive cascades called "The Four Falls," having a total descent of eighty feet.

Although the Aroostook waters are not well stocked with fish, the Tobique Indians succeed in spearing a good many salmon at the deep black pool below the fall. Some idea of that fish's strength and activity may be conveyed by merely stating that a few small salmon succeed in ascending the gorge. Of late years grilse have been taken with the fly at the mouth of the Little Machias River.

### THE TOBIQUE RIVER.

Not often does a river like the St. John, considerably exceeding four hundred miles in length, receive its two principal tributaries within a distance of four miles; yet just so far below Aroostook the famous Tobique River pours its pure, translucent waters into the greater stream. The Tobique measures about one hundred and ten miles to the source of the so-called Right Hand Branch, and drains fifteen hundred and sixty square miles. A gentleman visiting the river in 1863 says: "The mouth of the Tobique is exceedingly insignificant, and entirely unsuggestive of the beautiful scenery which characterizes the river in every other part. This unprepossessing appearance is caused by the land being here quite low, and the channel obstructed by evergreen intervale islands. One would scarcely suppose that there was any river here at all, much less one of the largest tributaries of the river St. John." To-day the water rushes forth in one rapidly moving mass, which presents an imposing appearance, even when viewed from the Andover bank. Can lumber, swift water, and ice, in so short a period, have completely eroded these " evergreen intervale inlands," and scattered them, in the form of silt, along miles of the river below ?

The Tobique and St. John waters do not thoroughly intermingle where they meet, but even at Andover, two miles down, the former stream's proximity is indicated by the transparency of the river near the eastern bank. Below Green River the line of demarcation is equally distinct.

On " The Point," above the Tobique outlet, we find a village peopled exclusively by Maliseet Indians, the aboriginal proprietors of both the Tobique and St. John. There are three principal Maliseet villages, — one at St. Mary's, opposite Fredericton; one on the west bank of the St. John, twelve miles above Fredericton, and the one under consideration. A family of the Penobscot tribe has settled at St. Pamphile, near Big Black

River, and a few scattered Maliseet families live at Edmundston and other points. Here, as elsewhere, these dusky aborigines are incapable of thorough civilization, but peaceful and inoffensive nevertheless. Some of them farm in a small way; all have ceased to live in wigwams. The men build canoes, hunt, and act as guides. The squaws make baskets and like articles of commerce, and indeed do all the less interesting work, as no disturbing modern theories of woman's rights have entered the cerebral cavity of the brawny Maliseet. In every village the Indians maintain a brood of ugly, vicious dogs; but dogs not under their immediate control they greatly fear. The birch-bark canoe is used invariably, while the French and English settlers along the Upper St. John prefer the pirogue, a clumsy-looking craft, shaped, like that of the ancient Britons, from a single log. In still water the birch outstrips the pirogue, especially in running with the wind, but in poling rapids the pirogue keeps the better headway. The Indians experience some difficulty at present in procuring suitable bark for canoe-building. The white or canoe birch is said to attain a diameter of six or seven feet in some parts of the northern woods, but so widespread has been its destruction that the Indian is compelled to seek it in regions growing ever more remote. Where once canoes were covered with a single sheet of bark, they now too often exhibit unbecoming seams and patches, which, opening from atmospheric change or contact with stones and snags, necessitate a frequent use of the rosin-pot.

Two lakes resting on the common watershed between the St. John and Miramichi rivers, and called respectively " Long " and " Trousers," form the principal sources of the Tobique. Trousers Lake, which is five miles long, has been named from the similarity in form to a well-known article of male attire. Had nature placed it on the broad Aroostook they would have called it " Pants." The shores are low and thickly wooded to the water's edge with black spruce, which imparts a weird and gloomy aspect. Long Lake, seven miles in length, is much more beautiful, with higher shores. Large bowlders, deeply overgrown with moss, cover the surface of the country in this vicinity. Both lakes send forth goodly streams, which, by uniting, create the " Right Hand Branch," or principal water, of the Tobique. Geographically speaking, it is the " left hand branch," but popular names, when generally accepted, admit of no correction. From Long Lake a portage of seven miles leads to the upper waters of the Little Southwest Miramichi River; a very difficult portage to cross, but one that affords the traveler what is possibly the longest and most attractive journey through an unbroken wilderness to be found east of the St. Lawrence. Britt Brook, a tributary of the Long

Lake stream, flows from a little lake on the same watershed with the others.

The Right Hand Branch has a rough fall, three or four feet high, six miles above its junction with the Left Hand Branch, Little Tobique, or Nictaux; and elsewhere is rapid and ledgy, with high banks, gradually rising below the mouth of the Don River, or Long Lake stream. Above the Don the bowlders make the channel rough and difficult to navigate.

The Serpentine River enters from the east, about twelve miles below the Don, and widens at one part to form Serpentine Lake, a very tortuous sheet of water, surrounded by hills which decline to form flat projecting headlands. The channel is incumbered by bowlders for six miles below the lake, and then we find a deadwater approached by lofty ridges which stretch away towards Cow Mountain, on the southeast. Nine miles below the deadwater the river cuts through a granite belt, forming rapids and falls, around which a portage of a quarter of a mile becomes necessary. Several large brooks enter, and most of them, including North Pole Brook, rise near the sources of the Little Southwest Branch of the Nepisiguit. The various lakes we have mentioned lie approximately parallel with each other, and are connected by a series of portages; that from Serpentine Lake to Britt Brook Lake being the longest.

The word Nictaux means " Forks," and in no

other part of the country do we find such a peculiar corrivation as the Nictaux or Forks of the Tobique. Almost at the confluence of the two principal streams, the Mamozekel River enters the Right Hand Branch; the Sisson stream, the Left. The same explorer who noted the islands near the mouth remarked: "The two branches form with the main stream a figure somewhat resembling an italic T."

The Sisson Branch has a fall seven miles above the mouth, where a portage of more than a mile must be made; above the fall a tributary enters from the northeast, flowing from Sisson Lake, an excellent water for trout. A lessee of the Tobique, accustomed to hunt around the Nictaux with John Bernard and "Frank," two of the most experienced Indians at "The Point," says: "Up to the present time (March, 1893), no person, not even a lumberman or Indian, has ever visited the headwaters of the main Sisson stream." There can be little question about the accuracy of his information.

The Nictaux, or Little Tobique, runs about thirty-five miles and drains, with the Sisson Branch, an area of three hundred and seventy square miles. The drainage area of the Right Hand Branch is slightly greater. All these streams spread out over the country so as to give a fan-shaped appearance when viewed on the map, the main Tobique being the handle of the fan, the various branches the spokes. The many lakes, ponds, and barren lands around the outskirts of the watershed afford a hunting ground for moose and other large game, very little, if any, inferior to that surrounding the upper Aroostook.

Nictaux Lake, the most picturesque little water imaginable, and the head of the Left Hand Branch, nestles at the base of Bald Mountain, the highest peak in New Brunswick. The mountain, which is not, strictly speaking, bald, but clothed with a stunted vegetation, rises quite abruptly from the water's edge to a height of 2,240 feet, or a little less than half a mile. The sides are strewn with large detached blocks of granite, and the slope has been ascertained, by actual measurement, to be no less than forty-five degrees. The view from the summit is so extensive that on a clear day with a good glass one may on the one hand see the cliffs of Gaspé to the northward, and on the other, in the far-off south, the still more lofty and snow-crowned peak of Katahdin. The whole country, as far as the eye can reach, is one unbroken wilderness, thrown into mountains and ridges of every variety of outline. A stream having a few feet of rapid descent divides Nictaux Lake into two parts, the upper part connecting with Nepisiguit Lake by a portage two miles and a half long. By ascending the Tobique, crossing this portage, and descending the Nepisiguit River, the traveler will enjoy a very surfeit of good hunting and fishing,

rapid-shooting, beautiful scenery, and wild camp
life. The lower lake is two miles long by one
broad, and completely inclosed by hills, except at
the ends. A tiny island, bare of all vegetation,
rises in the 'very centre of the eastern end, immediately beneath Bald Mountain, affording the
jaded traveler a complete refuge from those
quintessences of wickedness on wings, the black
flies.

The Little Tobique is somewhat obstructed by
rapids for a few miles below the lake, and then
becomes narrow, deep, and swift, with many wind-
ings. The Great and Little Cedar streams enter
from the north, their upper waters being probably
as little known as those of the Sisson Branch.
Below "The Cedars" the stream becomes more
tortuous than ever, the current slower, the banks
thickly overgrown with tangled alders. Had the
ancients been familiar with Northern New Brunswick they might have chosen the Nictaux or
Cabineau, instead of the Meander, as an illustration of thoroughly aimless crookedness.

The main Tobique measures some sixty-three
miles from the Nictaux to Indian Point, the only
really rough waters occurring at the Narrows and
Red Rapids, although the current is swift in most
places. The valley is one of the most fertile and
beautiful ones in the Province, and on no other
tributary of the St. John, unless it is the Aroostook, has the pristine forest so rapidly disappeared

before the settler's axe. While in 1860 but a few scattered dwellings appeared, near the Red Rapids, the valley is now continuously, in many places thickly, settled from the Nictaux to the St. John.

One of the most enchanting parts of the stream is the Blue Mountain Bend, where the water is smooth, deep, and transparently clear, and the three ragged summits of the Blue Mountains rise abruptly on the east. The soil is reddish below Two Brooks; the land alluvial and rich. There are many islands, low and covered with luxuriant vegetation. Dr. Gesner estimates their number in the main Tobique to be no less than seventy, but it is liable to change from time to time through natural causes.

The Gulquac enters the Tobique from the south, about twenty-five miles below the Nictaux, and Gulquac Lake, the source of the south and principal branch, is connected with Trousers Lake by a portage two miles and one half long. The stream is rather too rough for canoeing, as it winds around the bases of bold and rugged cliffs, but the upper waters of both branches lie well within the country of large game. In the summer of 1885 the industrious beaver so far forgot his constitutional dislike of civilization as to construct a dam across it, four miles from the settlements in the Tobique valley, a perfect model of infra-human architecture by which every drop of water was successfully turned into the adjoining woods, and the river bed left quite dry for many yards below. " Beaver like white man," remarked the delighted guide on first discovering it, " settles down and goes to work ; otter like Injun, here to-day, there to-morrow."

The Au-kee-awe-waps-ke-he-gan, or " River with a wall at its mouth," is another principal contributor of the Tobique, entering from the south, twenty-eight miles above Indian Point. Its name, which certainly deserves to have some meaning, has been successively shortened to " Wapskehegan" and " Wapsky," while the " wall at the mouth " consists of a cliff of red and snow-white gypsum, interstratified with marl and sandstone, and often of a pearly whiteness. It is sixty feet high, and nearly perpendicular, exhibiting a curious and beautiful appearance, from the alternating bands of gypsum and red sandstone. The Wapsky, with its tributary the Rivière du Chute, and the Southwest Miramichi River, have interlocking waters. Possibly a canoe could be " portaged" across, although the task would doubtless be very difficult.

Three Brooks stream flows from the north, a few miles below the apex of the Wapsky Flat. On the east branch we discover an excellent trout pool. The Otella or Odell River flows from the south, its two principal branches uniting in a picturesque ravine, where the country is dotted with curious little mounds, almost exactly pyramidal in form.

An interesting feature of the lower Tobique is the almost tropical luxuriance of the vegetation. On the banks are elms and mountain ash of enormous height, with tall grass, and ferns four or five feet high. Even the extreme severity of the winters seems unable to check the natural outgrowth of soils so fertile. At the Red Rapids, twelve miles above the mouth, where beds of bright red sandstone cross obliquely the bed of the stream, we find the only rough water that the canoeist need encounter, except the rapids in the narrows; but while difficult to ascend by poling, the Red Rapids are not at all dangerous. An Indian guide, inclined to be lazy, — and how many Indian guides are not? — likes to make the most of them as an excuse for shortening the day's journey and protracting his employment.

Within a circle, having a twelve-mile radius, we find the Grand Falls of the St. John, the Aroostook Fall, and the Tobique Narrows, three lasting monuments of the glacial era. It is probable that, immediately after the disturbance which turned the rivers from their respective channels, three mighty cataracts were formed, situated at the lower ends of the modern gorges, and equal to their present massive walls in height. A process of erosion began, continued through the countless ages, a very race of waterfalls, a never-ceasing

struggle to wear away the barriers of rock. With
what result? The Grand Falls have moved one
mile and lost one half their height and majesty.
The Aroostook, moving too speedily, has formed
a series of cascades, which being less in power
will long remain there. The Tobique, least in
volume while greatest in erosive might, alone has
conquered the impeding barrier, and now it gam-
bols over the vanquished ledges in some rather
lively rapids, the sole remaining remnants of the
great post-glacial cataract. In a few more ages
the narrows will undoubtedly present the placid
surface of a lake. The obstruction which created
Grand Falls stemmed back the water above, but
the similar impediment which caused the Tobique
Narrows merely heaped up large quantities of
traveling sand in what is called "The Grand
Bar," the water plainly increasing instead of diminishing in speed. Canoes may descend the narrows with safety, although the novice sometimes
experiences such an uprising of the hair as would
put "the fretful porcupine" to shame; and the
stream drivers steer small rafts down during the
spring floods. Within the lower and middle portions of the gorge the water is tranquil and very
deep, but so beautifully transparent that the in-
terlacing veins of pure white calcite may be seen
distinctly at a depth of sixty feet, contrasting, as
they do, so strongly with the darker ledges of
slate.

The reader may be disappointed to learn that
the public are debarred from using the Tobique
as other than a natural highway. Such is the
case, however, the local government having leased
it for salmon and trout fishing to the same syndi-
cate that controls Green River. Without discus-
sing the propriety of this mode of raising provincial revenue, we merely remark that the policy
has caused much ill feeling on the Tobique. So
general was the discontent at first, that when some
poachers fired upon a fishing party, instantly
killing the wife of one of the lessees, the sympa-
thetic jurymen could not be convinced that the
crime was one of higher degree than manslaughter.
The great salmon pools of the Tobique are distributed along the river as follows, viz.: Four on
the Serpentine, at distances almost equally apart,
dividing that river into four equal sections; two
within the first mile and a half of the Right Hand
Branch below the confluence of the streams flowing from Long and Trousers lakes; one on the
Right Hand Branch about three miles above the
Serpentine; two close together and perhaps five
miles below the Serpentine; one, called the Seven
Mile Pool, it being just that distance above the
Nictaux; one about half a mile above the Mamozekel; one at the Nictaux or Forks; one at the
mouth of Cedar Brook on the Little Tobique;
one two miles and one four miles below the Nictaux; one just above Riley Brook, and one a mile

and a half below Riley Brook: seventeen in all.
Of course salmon may be taken at many other
places, and in addition to the generally good trout
fishing there are pools of special excellence on
the Serpentine, three miles below the lake, and
on the main Tobique at the mouth of a small
brook entering from the south, a little below
Gulquac. Trousers Lake and another small lake
near by are also considered good waters for trout.
The Tobique salmon is smaller than the Restigouche, and less gamey than the Miramichi
salmon, but affords very good sport nevertheless.
A gentleman when visiting the river in 1863
said: "The trout are so numerous and voracious
as to jump at the canoe paddles;" while in 1842 a
settler living near the mouth killed twelve barrels
of salmon with a single spear. Those happy days
have long gone by, and with civilization's onward
march the whole basin of the St. John is rapidly
deteriorating as a country for fish and game.

### STATISTICS.

The total drainage area of the St. John River
above Andover is about 13,200 square miles.
This estimate is somewhat reduced by excluding
the Allagash above the Chamberlain dam. Considering the South or Baker Branch as the principal source, all the tributaries entering on the
left-hand side drain collectively 7,617 square
miles, all tributaries entering from the right-

hand side 5,488 square miles. It is a peculiar feature of the system that fourteen large tributaries enter from the left side, and only three, the Allagash, Fish, and Aroostook rivers, from the right. All the streams having pure transparent water are in the first group.

The basin of the St. John in Maine covers 7,638 square miles, or about one fourth the land surface of the State.

Mr. Walter Wells, superintendent of the hydrographic survey in Maine, estimates the mean annual discharge of the Aroostook at 81,900,000,-000 cubic feet, and the discharges of the Great Fish and Allagash rivers at 34,710,000,000 and 57,720,000,000 cubic feet respectively, while the whole basin of the St. John in Maine sheds 284,-000,000,000 cubic feet of water annually. The Aroostook basin is computed to contain 59.95 square miles of lake surface, Squapan Lake (superficial area 10 square miles) being the largest body of water; the Allagash basin 120.90 square miles, Chamberlain (20 square miles) being the largest lake; Fish River basin 89 square miles, with individual lake areas as follows, viz.: Long Lake, 19 square miles; Square Lake, 15; Eagle Lake, 22; Nadeau Lake, 5.50; Portage Lake, 8.50; and Great Fish Lake, 7 square miles; the St. Francis basin, 36.65 square miles; and the whole St. John basin in Maine, 350 square miles. By the Chamberlain dam the flowage of 36 square miles of the Allagash lakes is turned southeasterly into the Penobscot River.

## FROM ANDOVER TO WOODSTOCK.

Between Andover and Woodstock (fifty miles) the St. John winds about from east to west, and west to east, in a series of gentle curves, the general course remaining north and south. It is everywhere a moderately deep and very swiftly flowing river, not varying greatly in width except where the channel separates to inclose an island. Many natural terraces are found, often forming banks of gravel and sand from thirty to fifty feet high; elsewhere the hills slope up from the water's edge to a considerable height. On both terraces and slopes the land is fertile and under cultivation. From the summit of Moose Mountain, a rugged peak, over eight hundred feet high, in the vicinity of the Muniac stream, deriving its name from a resemblance, when viewed at a distance, to the body and hornless head of a moose, a magnificent view may be obtained of the river, winding, for many miles, like a silvery streak, through a country so patched with dark spruce forest, and cultivated tracts of a lighter green, as to give the whole scene the appearance of a gigantic chess-board. A similar view is obtained from Stickney Brook ridge, nearly opposite Florenceville.

Andover village, which consists of a long row

of pleasant cottages near the brink of a terrace overlooking the river and the picturesquely wooded ridge that rises abruptly from the opposite bank, is the dividing point between the English and French civilizations of Western New Brunswick. Having passed it, on our downward voyage, we find the settled country not so much confined to the river valley as hitherto, but extending for many miles to the eastward and westward. A branch of the Canadian Pacific Railway follows the east bank quite closely, utilizing the level table lands on the natural terraces. The principal villages along the river are Kent, Florenceville, Hartland, and Upper Woodstock, while Glassville, Centreville, and other small distributing centres are scattered over " the back country." At the mouth of Hardwood Creek there is a village bearing the unpoetical name of " Bumfraw," a rather humorous corruption of the French " *bois franche*." Upper Woodstock is called " Hardscrabble," rather ridiculously, because it is a " hard scrabble," or difficult and laborious task, to ascend a rapid below it.

In the first few miles below Andover, large masses of rock, seemingly detached, rise here and there above the river's surface, but they are not surrounded by rough water. The current is swift everywhere, but most rapid at " Fitz Herbert's Rips " (between the two Guisiguit rivers), on the channels surrounding Green Island, above the Big

Presque Isle River, and from the Little Presque
Isle to Hartland Bar.

The principal streams entering from the west
are the Rivière du Chute, the Upper and Lower
Guisiguit, and the Big and Little Presque Isle
rivers; the principal ones entering from the east
are the Muniac, Monquart, Shikitehawk, and Beccaguimec rivers. The Rivière du Chute is a
small stream of very clear water, with a natural
fall at the mouth, the height of which has been
reduced from sixty to eight feet by long-continued
erosive action. The Monquart and Shikitehawk
are also transparently clear, and should be good
for trout, but they rise in a very mountainous
country near the sources of the Odell River
(a branch of the Tobique) and the Southwest
Branch of the Miramichi, and are too shallow and
rocky for a convenient ascent by canoe. There
is a rather picturesque ravine and fall on the
Shikitehawk, and at Kent Station, near its mouth,
an excellent portage road, but sixteen miles in
length, connects the St. John River with the
Miramichi at Foreston. The Miramichi is a
famous salmon stream, and many sportsmen use
this road annually as an easy way of reaching it.
The Big Presque Isle River (not to be confounded
with its namesake on the Aroostook) is a goodly
stream of clear and rapid water, running forty
miles, and more or less navigable by canoe for
half that distance. It winds around Mars Hill,

of international celebrity, which is the highest mountain on the middle St. John (1,600 feet), and commands an unrivaled view of the country. Two miles below Hartland the Little Pokiok stream emerges from a cavernous cleft in the rocks. In fact, many minor brooks along this part of the river, and Acker Brook especially, flow for some distance through deep ravines.

Woodstock (4,500) is the third city in size and commercial importance within the St. John River valley. It contains many pleasing private residences, but no very noteworthy public buildings, and is the trade centre for the populous agricultural districts of Carleton County.

### THE BECCAGUIMEC RIVER.

At Hartland village, twelve miles above Woodstock, the Beccaguimec River enters the St. John from the east, a stream, that is, in its general course, the most crooked of all the tributaries, while having a greater descent between source and mouth than any other branch of equal length. It is more or less " canoeable " for seventeen or eighteen miles, the rapid descent being largely caused by a few falls on the north branch; and the Coldstream, a tributary, is also navigable at medium water. The north and south branches flow from opposite directions for fifteen miles above their junction, and then their valleys gradually approach until at their heads they overlap.

" Guimec " Lake, the source of the south branch, is small but picturesque, and most easily reached from Millville, a station on the Canadian Pacific Railway.

In 1885 two geological explorers attempted to reach " Guimec " Lake by wading up the stream. Toiling onward, now in the water, now in the neighboring swamps, while the miserable brook dwindled down to microscopical proportions, they reached a great morass, and still no lake in sight. A rain came on, no light one, and unable to return by reason of approaching darkness, supperless, shelterless, wet and worn, they stretched upon a heap of rotten wood, composing their weary limbs for sleeplessness. When morning dawned they rose much unrefreshed, and shaking off the ants and centipedes set forth for Millville. It was a most inglorious retreat.

The Beccaguimec water is pure and clear, and the trout fishing on the north branch probably the best obtainable between Andover and Fredericton.

### THE MEDUXNIKEAG RIVER.

The Meduxnikeag River (drainage area about 420 square miles), which unites with the St. John at Woodstock, is formed by the junction of two streams of nearly equal size twelve miles above the mouth, one flowing southerly from the Aroostook watershed, the other northerly through one of the richest farming districts of Maine. Houlton, an ambitious rival of Woodstock, and the metropolis of Aroostook County, is situated on the south branch. Its business section is clustered about an open square, from which pleasant residential streets extend in several directions.

In the more remote country districts above Grand Falls, the watercourses afford the most convenient or only routes for travel; consequently the degree of each stream's "navigability" is a matter of common knowledge; but below Andover the country is so covered by a network of roads, that a person interested in any stream whose current it requires a more or less experienced poler to overcome, rather prefers to walk or drive there than to incur fatigue and strain his canoe in the arduous exercise of swinging the pole. Especially is this true of the Meduxnikeag, but the possible canoeist may be interested in learning that there is a waterfall near the forks, and a very pretty valley from there to Woodstock.

### FROM WOODSTOCK TO FREDERICTON.

Quite various are the aspects which the river presents between Woodstock and Fredericton, a distance of sixty-three miles. Above Eel River the current is everywhere swift, the channel often splitting to inclose an alluvial island. Indeed, we find no islands in the St. John above Belleisle Bay which are not composed purely of alluvium, or glacial drift. The hills reach a considerable altitude on both sides of the valley, although the immediate river banks are neither as uniformly abrupt nor as stony as in the vicinity of Monquart and Muniac ; hence affording better facilities for camping. The scenery is decidedly picturesque, especially for ten miles below Woodstock and the same distance above Fredericton. A granite belt crosses the valley between the Eel and Nacawick rivers, and as no geological formation roughens a country like a granite one, whether granite *in situ* or granite superficially distributed by glacial action, the river becomes obstructed by ledges and loose lying drift, over which the water pours in a rapid called the Meductic Fall. Canoes may descend without inconvenience by keeping well to the right-hand bank, and the Woodstock steamer ascends at high water. In fact the Meductic is a mere pigmy when compared with such aquatic toboggan slides as endanger navigation above the Allagash. Below the fall the river is more sluggish and much deeper, with a maximum depth of fifty-four feet at Pokiok Eddy, measured at low water. There was an ancient fort above Meductic, on the west bank, and near it an Indian burial ground, the site of which is now overgrown by hawthorn-trees.

The sharpest and most peculiar twist in the river channel below Grand Falls is the Nackawick Bend, after rounding which the stream runs perfectly straight for eighteen miles in a wide

and shallow bed filled with islands. People
sometimes call this straight course the Upper
Reach, as it is of equal length with the Long
Reach below Gagetown, although quite unlike
in every other respect. The shallow waters and
sand-bars, though accompanied by a quickening
of the current, allow teams to ford the channel
in various places during the summer months.
Horses would probably have to swim some distance in crossing elsewhere below Edmundston,
unless at the great bar near Hartland. At the
foot of the Upper Reach the river turns again,
at an exact right angle; a whirlpool, known
as Burgoyne's Eddy, forming at high water,
near the right-hand bank. The current slackens
very much, and the water for nine miles is as
deep as in the narrow channel below Meductic;
then the whole appearance of the river changes
once more. The Keswick stream enters from the
north, ten miles above Fredericton, and below it
the river bed is literally choked with islands of
all dimensions, and divided into innumerable
channels of varying width, depth, and rapidity.
High hills, higher than any we have seen below
Eel River, uprise on both sides, their slopes being in great part under cultivation. From the
various summits, and more especially from Rock-
land Hill, a view of the closely clustered Keswick
Islands is obtained, such as is ever appreciated,
and rarely forgotten. At Sugar Island, the

largest of the group, the St. John measures two
miles and a half from bank to bank, its greatest
width above Fredericton. Savage Island, the
second in area, was a famous rendezvous of the
Maliseets in early days, and here they are said to
have been attacked by the restless Mohawks, who
descended the river for scalps and glory. A
bird's-eye view of the island may be had from
Clarke's or Currie's Mountain, a detached precipitous peak, with a ravine behind, where many
more of our inoffensive Maliseets became pre-
maturely bald at the touch of the keen-edged
tomahawk, unless tradition lies. All the islands
are low, grassy, and fringed with elm-trees and
bushes, and, excepting a few small portions of
them, annually submerged by the spring floods.
The few dry spots are little hummocks, formed
from nothing more durable than the common
alluvium, on which early settlers and adventurous
farmers built houses occasionally in years gone
by. How they must have enjoyed the spectacle
of the spring ice roaring, grinding, and crunching
on every side, and momentarily threatening to
pile against their little cottages and sweep them
ruthlessly down-stream! For three days, at least,
these farmers on the knolls, provided they had
missed the last opportunity of reaching the main
land, must have moved in a social circle exclusively confined to members of their own families, — a sufficient time to enable our friend, Mr.

Harvey, to reach civilization from his log house on the Allagash. Between Sugar and Savage islands the principal body of the water shifts from the southwest to the northeast side of the valley, through a channel called the Grand Passage, but it gradually returns before reaching Fredericton.

The extraordinary tides of the Bay of Fundy influence the river as far as Chapel Bar, above Spring Hill, so we find no more swift currents. On this account the Fredericton canoeists are better accustomed to the paddle than the pole.

### MINOR TRIBUTARIES BELOW WOODSTOCK.

We now return to Woodstock to see what tributarial contributions the St. John receives between that city and Fredericton. The principal ones, briefly enumerated, are as follows: from the left-hand side, Gibson's Mill Stream, and the Nackawick, Koack, Mactaquac, Keswick, and Nashwaaksis rivers; from the right-hand side, Bull's Creek, the Eel, Shogomoc, and Pokiok rivers, and Upper Garden's and Long's creeks. The highest fall in the St. John River system, to the writer's knowledge and belief, is that called Hay's Fall, on a small brook entering the main river midway between Bull's Creek and Eel River. Here the water takes a perpendicular leap of ninety feet from a rugged cliff, at the brow and base of which good views may be obtained. A thick growth of tall spruces and firs adds picturesqueness, but the stream is unfortunately so small as to disappear entirely in the summer season, when the fall dwindles gradually down to a collection of wet and dripping moss.

Gibson's Mill Stream is very much larger, and the narrows, three miles above the mouth, containing a series of rough cascades flanked by perpendicular cliffs of a great but as yet unmeasured height, will repay a visit at any time. As was noted of Acker Brook, above Woodstock, a very small stream may have a very deep valley of erosion, a fact again illustrated by the presence of a deep ravine midway between Eel and Shogomoc rivers, where the little Sullivan's Creek trickles out to the St. John. So the small Koack River has eroded a chasm so dark and cavernous that all attempts to take photographs within are said to fail through insufficiency of light. The shadows of lofty firs and spruces contribute materially to the gloom of this romantic spot. Within the chasm there is a fall, perhaps eighty feet in height. Upper and Lower Garden's and Kelly's creeks all have picturesque falls, and they were tolerably good trout brooks some years ago. The Mactaquac is somewhat larger, and has two principal tributaries, one flowing from Scotch Lake in Queensbury. Its lower valley presents an attractive appearance, but the upper waters are rarely visited by sportsmen, and probably unattainable by canoe in the fishing season.

## EEL RIVER.

Eel River rises in a small pond, called the Third Eel River Lake, near Skiff Lake, the source of a branch of the St. Croix. It drains an area of two hundred and thirty square miles, probably deriving its name from the crooked course it takes while doing so. The first of the three Eel River lakes is the largest, receiving the overflow of the second through a small unnavigable stream of very rapid descent. From the first lake to Benton village navigation by canoe is comparatively easy, although short portages are necessary around two waterfalls, one a few miles below the lake, the other at Dinnen's Mill, above the mouth of a tributary oddly named Pok'o'moonshine Brook. Some people say that "Pok'o'moonshine" is of Indian origin, and others that "pok" is an abbreviation of "poke," meaning a ray, as a "poke of light." The existence of a lake called Sunpoke on the Oromocto River has a decided tendency to support the latter view. In early times Eel River was a much used thoroughfare between the St. John and the St. Croix, a portage of three miles, called Metagmuckschesh, connecting it with North Lake, the head of the Chiputnetecook chain. Metagmuckschesh has been a great Indian road for centuries, various reputable writers asserting that the flat rocks (a coarse granite), over which the narrow file of Indians passed, have been worn

to a depth of several inches by the tread of moc-
casined feet.   Mr. Frederick Kidder, in his work
on "Military operations in Eastern Maine and
Nova Scotia during the Revolution," says of this
pathway: "It has undoubtedly been used for
many centuries, and may be pronounced the most
ancient evidence of mankind in New England."
In 1777, Col. John Allen, attended by about five
hundred Indians and colonists, a majority of whom
were women and children, ascended Eel River and
crossed Metagmuckshcesh to North Lake, depart-
ing from Fort Meductic on the 13th day of July.
The lower course of Eel River is obstructed by
falls and rapids, on which account the Indians carried their canoes overland from Meductic to Benton (five miles) when journeying westward from
the St. John to the St. Croix and Matawamkeag
via Metagmuckschesh, but frequently descended
the stream when traveling the opposite way.

The pickerel, a veritable fresh - water shark,
seems to have received in the First Eel River Lake
its primary introduction to the waters of the St.
John, whence it has spread over all the lower tributaries, wherever the current is sluggish, proving
an inveterate foe to many other fishes, more especially to trout.   Its fondness for the trout probably arises from the fact of their being scaleless,
and consequently more "swallowable."    Luckily
the pickerel dislikes rapid water, and is seldom
found in the St. John above Eel River.

## THE SHOGOMOC RIVER.

The Shogomoc River, although within the region of granite, is navigable from a short distance above the mouth. At the mouth we find it a most tumultuous torrent, rushing among, and tumbling over, a typical collection of ledges and granitic bowlders. There are innumerable lakes on the stream (Great Shogomoc Lake being very much the largest), and several of them are abundantly stocked with trout. The Shogomoc rises near the Palfrey Mountains, and Canterbury Station, on the Woodstock branch of the Canadian Pacific Railway, is the most convenient starting point for persons desirous of visiting the upper waters.

## THE POKIOK RIVER.

The word " Pokiok " is said to mean " narrow opening," and we certainly find on this river a very narrow opening. Barely twenty-five feet apart, but from fifty to seventy feet high, and accurately perpendicular, are the dark red granite walls that inclose the Pokiok near its confluence with the St. John. Within this strange chasm the water makes a series of leaps, aggregating about seventy-five feet in height, and roars and foams most furiously. In the flood season the scene presented is intensely picturesque, more especially as in driving along the Woodstock road one cannot see the ravine until almost directly over it. A sluiceway has been constructed for the passage of planks from the mill, down which an elderly "Pokiokean," whose valor is at least on a par with his discretion, rides frequently on floating timber, for the moderate remuneration of twenty-five cents per trip. When paddling down the St. John in early spring a blast of cold air is felt, which proceeds directly from the Pokiok gorge, and is laden with the peculiar odor of the fall.

The general course of the river, from the source in Lake George, is almost exactly parallel to that of the St. John, while the flow is in the opposite direction. By portaging five miles from Lower Prince William to the lake, a down-stream circuit can be made (similar to that of the Fish or Madawaska rivers, although much shorter), the stream being readily navigable for canoes, and quite sluggish in places.

Three "Pokioks" are found in the St. John River system. Two have the narrow opening which the name is said to signify, but the third, a brook entering the Tobique four miles above Indian Point, and not previously mentioned, has but a simple fall at the mouth, which I found by barometric observation to be forty-five feet in height.

### THE NACKAWICK RIVER.

The Nackawick River (drainage area one hundred and fifty square miles) enters the St. John from the northeast, three miles below Pokiok. It has three principal branches, all flowing from the same watershed that produces the Beccaguimec and Keswick rivers. A line of the Canadian Pacific Railway crosses two branches, and on the southeast or principal one we find Millville, an important centre for the local lumber trade. The Nackawick is unadapted for practical canoeing, and little would be gained by visiting the upper waters, except for the purpose of hooking small trout, which abound in most of them.

### THE KESWICK RIVER.

The valleys of the Keswick and Mactaquac are separated by Keswick Ridge, which terminates at the St. John River in a precipitous cliff called "The Peddler's Leap." The Keswick stream rises near Beccaguimec Lake, previously mentioned, and runs forty miles, emptying into the channel behind Sugar Island.

So well watered is the basin of the St. John, that it would be quite impossible to find a tract of land four miles square not traversed by some brook or rivulet, and several different rivers always flow from every well-defined watershed. Thus, in the case before us, the Keswick, Nackawick and Beccaguimec all rise in a locality the central point of which is twenty-five miles east of Woodstock, but the mouths of the Keswick and Beccaguimec are sixty-five miles apart, measured along the valley of the St. John. The common watershed is an undulating country, traversed here and there by well-defined ridges, dotted with small lakes, and clad in a luxuriant greenwood forest. It is the border of New Brunswick's greatest wilderness, a vast region, untenanted by other than the *feræ naturæ* of our common law, extending northeastward, without a break, to the Intercolonial Railway and the valley of the Restigouche River.

The Keswick's principal branches unite twenty-two miles from the mouth of the stream, and below their confluence the valley gradually widens, finally becoming a fertile and thickly inhabited farming country. Two large tributaries enter from the east. The stream is navigable by canoe, except in the dry season, with just enough rough water to make things cheerful; and the railway follows nearly all its countless meanderings. It is not prominent among the fishing rivers, but small trout abound in the upper waters.

### THE NASHWAAKSIS RIVER.

The Nashwaaksis has three principal branches, all uniting within a third of a mile, after the fashion of the Touladi and Tobique, and below the

forks is navigable, generally speaking, when the
Keswick is. It contains many deep pools, which
would naturally harbor trout of very fair dimensions, but the small-boy crop in this vicinity is
large, and small boys, here as elsewhere, take
much delight in fishing. The east branch has a
very pretty symmetrical fall, about fourteen feet
high, with a deep and thickly wooded ravine below. Above the fall are the wild meadows, where
myriads of small trout are hooked every twenty-
fourth of May. McLeod's Bluff, a bold face of
volcanic rock with a huge talus at the base, over-
looks the stream below the forks, and for an
equal distance above the mouth the water is still,
and the banks overgrown with leafy trees that
cast their perfect reflections upon its surface.
Here the young "Frederictonian" paddles his
"best girl" on moonlight evenings, and the stilly
air is often laden with the murmur of suppressed
voices, blended with, and occasionally interrupted
by, the buzz of the unceremonious mosquito.

### FREDERICTON.

Emerging from the narrow opening of the Nashwaaksis we see before us the roofs and spires of .
Fredericton, the political, legal, and educational
centre of New Brunswick, second in industrial importance, and first in natural beauty of location,
of the various communities within the St. John
River valley. The site of the city is a flat dilu-

vial plain, two miles in length by one in width, laved by the river, and backed by wooded hills. The streets are broad and regular, those parallel with the water having been named after the reigning sovereigns at the time of the town's incorporation. Queen and King streets are nearest the river bank, Charlotte and George the most remote, and Brunswick in the centre, the group thus forming the combination: "Queen Charlotte (and) King George (of the house of) Brunswick."

Fredericton is justly termed "The Forest City" from the number and beauty of its shade trees. The elms attain a loftiness and graceful symmetry but rarely found, while willows of gigantic size adorn the water front in many places. Almost at the upper end of the flat, and opposite the Nashwaaksis, stands Government House, the official residence of nearly all New Brunswick's governors, an historic pile, thoroughly suggestive of the preconfederate aristocracy. The cathedral, a beautiful Gothic edifice, modeled after the parish church at Sandringham in England, is also near the river, while half way up the hill behind the town stands the University of New Brunswick, formerly, and much more appropriately, termed "King's College." Among the more historic buildings are the officers' barracks, which overlook a level willow-shaded lawn, much used in peace for tennis, and in war for drill.

The number and beauty of the landed estates

GOVERNMENT HOUSE, FREDERICTON

cannot fail to attract attention. Scattered about on plain and hillside, within the town, without the town, we find them everywhere: broad acres, spreading in grassy fields, and lawns, and fertile garden lots. Some tottering chimneys near the river bank denote the site of Rose Hall, a transitory asylum of the traitor Arnold subsequent to his discovery and inglorious northward flight; while at the western apex of the city flat, faced by the water, and shadowed by lofty pines, appears the ruined Hermitage.

Fredericton has been visited by several destructive conflagrations. In 1825 the Government House, with scores of shops and dwellings, was laid in ruins. The great fire of 1850 proved equally calamitous.

On the twenty-second day of February, 1785, Sir Guy Carleton made it the seat of government, when the ancient name "St. Anne's" was changed to "Frederick Town" in honor of His Royal Highness, the Bishop of Osnaburg.

### THE NASHWAAK RIVER.

The Nashwaak, running about seventy-five miles, and draining five hundred and eighty square miles, is somewhat larger than any tributary stream we have passed below the Tobique. It flows from St. Mary's Lake, a remote little body of water much more easily reached by a portage of a few miles from the valley of the Southwest Mira-

michi than by ascending the river to which it gives
rise. Indeed, it has been stated, by one familiar
with the successive explorations of Central New
Brunswick, that nobody ever succeeded in tracing
the Nashwaak stream upwards to the lake. This,
if true, is probably because the country in the
vicinity of the lake resembles that surrounding
the sources of the Napadogan stream, a principal
tributary, entering from the east, twelve miles
above Stanley. The writer visited the east branch
of the Napadogan in 1885, and found there some
extensive morasses, covered with a thick scrubby
growth, as difficult to walk through as deep snow,
and presenting a weird and gloomy appearance.
The stream was divided occasionally into several
channels, and the various members of the party
became separated, and were only united again
after much shouting and some hours spent in
struggling aimlessly through the swamp.

As instances of a curious nomenclature often
found in the St. John River system, we have
mentioned " Bumfraw " and " Pok'o'moonshine "
Brook, and the Nashwaak country is by no means
lacking in odd names. Thus one of the most
northerly tributaries, entering some ten miles
below the lake, is very comically named " Dough-
boy Brook " by the lumbermen, in commemora-
tion of a camp spree, when the men pelted each
other with no less adhesive a commodity than soft
dough. A few miles below this, where the river

abruptly changes course from south to east, enter
two streams which are spoken of collectively as
"The Sisters," but individually as "Miss Nashwaak" and "Sister Ann."

Fourteen miles above Stanley, a little lake
connects with the main Nashwaak by a short
thoroughfare, and immediately below the river is
dammed for lumbering purposes. In the pool
below the dam small trout are as numerous as
can be. At the Narrows, also, some seven miles
above, we may angle successfully for these sportive speckled beauties. There we find the roughest rapids on the river. The Napadogan stream,
which is one of the largest tributaries, flows
entirely within the wilderness, is navigable, but
not easily so, for canoes at medium water, and
abounds with small trout. Rocky Brook rises in
a bleak morass similar to that of the Napadogan.
Grand John Brook, which enters the Nashwaak
from the south, and bears the name of an old
Indian who hunted at one time on all these
waters, literally teems with small trout, but the
narrowness of the channel makes it difficult to
cast a fly with precision.

Civilization, that is to say settlement, has advanced thirty-four miles up the Nashwaak. At
Stanley village, which is picturesquely perched
on a hill slope, overlooking the valley, we find
some houses partially constructed with imported
timber, the people of old England formerly labor-

ing under a slight misapprehension regarding the extent of available woodland in the New World. Stanley has a population of five hundred, which is doubled on election days and other auspicious occasions.

Below Stanley the stream is everywhere navigable for canoes under ordinary conditions; the valley is continuously settled, and fully as picturesque as that of any other tributary of the St. John. Large trout frequent the stream, an occasional one turning the scales at three pounds; but the most experienced angler can never be sure of a catch, so shy are they. A famous pool is that at the mouth of Lower McBean's Brook. The river gradually increases in volume, receiving from the east the Budogan, or Cross Creek, the Undenack, or Upper McBean's Brook, Lower McBean's Brook, Manzer's Creek, and the Pennioc; and receiving from the west Tay Creek and the Dunbar or Cleuristic stream. The trout in Cross Creek and the Undenack are numerous, although quite small, but on the Tay, which is the longest tributary, and " canoeable " at certain times, a few large fish may be taken. Precipitate bluffs of sandstone crop out on the Undenack, above and below McKenzie's Brook, and in the talus beneath one of them, large but imperfect lepidodendrons and other fossilized plants of the Carboniferous era lie strewn about profusely. The Cleuristic divides two miles above the mouth, the principal branch being called Tin Kettle Brook, and one mile from the Nashwaak it has a very symmetrical fall, of similar dimensions to that on the east branch of the Nashwaaksis. The Pennioc is the most sluggish of all these waters, and navigable for canoes about eight miles, where it flows through a thickly-settled valley, possessed of much rural beauty. Once the stream excelled all others for trout fishing, except perhaps the Tay; and even now, overfished as it is, the angler occasionally becomes the happy possessor of a much larger trout than he ever even dreamed of catching there.

At the mouth of the Pennioc we find a very large alluvial island, strangely large to be inclosed by a river of no greater volume than the Nashwaak. Marysville, two miles below this, which is the metropolis of the Nashwaak valley, is a thoroughly one-man place, as much so as Pullman, Illinois, its mushroom growth being entirely due to the enterprise of Mr. Gibson, who controls the Nashwaak lumber trade and manufactures cotton. A strange contrast is presented by the high brick walls of the cotton-mill, backed, as they are, by a greenwood forest which extends without a break to the horizon, a very sea of conical treetops. Indeed, a straight line may be drawn through this forest from a point two miles from Fredericton that will not cross any road or settlement between the St. John River valley and the Intercolonial Railway, and a similar line from the northwest branch of the Nashwaaksis to the Restigouche River. It would be interesting to compare the area of this huge wilderness with that of the similar one surrounding the sources of the St. John and Allagash rivers.

The Nashwaak was said to be, many years ago, navigable for wood boats below Marysville, and subsequently shallowed by deposits of silt and sawdust. Newspapers of 1860 mourn the deterioration of the once excellent trout fishing off the bar at the mouth, where now the water is barely deep enough to float a canoe in midsummer. Certainly there would be as much wisdom to-day in trying to shoot a mastodon on the upper Pennioc as in attempting to capture trout with a fly off Nashwaak Bar.

At Heron Lake, two and one half miles from Fredericton, some interesting glacial phenomena may be seen. The water now flows into the Nashwaaksis, but the lake is merely held in place by a narrow and steep-sided moraine of glacial drift, separating it from a deeply-wooded ravine that extends eastward into the Nashwaak valley. Probably Heron Lake was once the source of Hot Water Creek, a tortuous little stream branching from the Nashwaak half a mile above the mouth, with deep sluggish water, where perch and pickerel roam in shoals, sheltering beneath the grass and lily-pads.

# CHAPTER IV.

## THE LOWER ST. JOHN.

### FROM FREDERICTON TO GAGETOWN.

THE physical features of the St. John alter greatly in the thirty-four miles between Fredericton and Gagetown. Nowhere else is the surrounding land so low, and on the east a mere alluvial flat of great extent separates its waters from those drained by the Jemseg. Every indication shows that this country was once the bed of a great lake, nearly triangular in form, with its apex at Salmon River and its base line along the valley of the St. John. The greatest length and breadth of the lake must have been about the same, as the distance from Nashwaak to Jemseg (thirty-five miles) nearly equals that from Oromocto to the head of the lowland on Salmon River. A log, in a perfect state of preservation, was discovered at a depth of twenty-four feet from the surface of this alluvium bed, about opposite Oromocto, and, as twenty feet is the difference to-day between the top of the flat and low-water mark, it would seem to have been deposited at a time when sediment first began to form in the old lake basin. Who can say what portion of the rock eroded from the several gorges of the St. John, Aroostook, and Tobique now enters into the composition of the Maugerville flat? There were a few, if not many, islands in the ancient lake, including the cup-shaped wooded mound below the Nashwaak. The currents of the St. John, flowing southeasterly, met those of the Grand Lake watershed, flowing southwesterly, and the most natural place for the deposit of silt and detritus was along the line of their junction, where we find the fluviatile deposits of to-day. Maugerville and Sheffield parishes are among the earliest settled districts on the St. John; the land is exceedingly rich, and annually manured by the silt-bearing freshets. It is an extraordinary fact that some of the farmers obtain a crop of vegetables and a crop of fish from the same piece of ground annually.

The current is sluggish at low-water, but everywhere perceptible, between Chapel Bar and Gagetown, and naturally, on nearing the coast, the ebb and flow of the fresh-water tide increases. In most, if not all, rivers of any volume, with estuary mouths, the current is continued much beyond the point of tide level by the pressure of water above, and what has been said of the St. John is strikingly true, on a much larger scale, of the Amazon and Congo.

The village of Oromocto, although small, is the shire-town of Sunbury County. Travelers say that the potato is the current medium of exchange there, but this is hearsay, and needs verification.

Oromocto was anciently an Indian resort, and the husbandman sometimes exposes a grave, or implements of stone and pottery, while working in the field. The Burton court-house, a few miles below the village, commands an unrivaled view of the river, with the great intervale islands, and the Maugerville flat beyond.

Gagetown, diminutive as it is, was, until recently, one of the largest communities in eastern North America unconnected with the outside world by rail or telegraph. In front flows Gagetown Creek, a sluggish stream connecting Hart's and Coy's lakes with the river. Grimross Neck, between the river and creek, has now become Grimross Island by the excavation of a short canal, which, if we except the canal connecting Telos Lake with Webster Brook on the Penobscot, and Morrow's little " dugway " on the Oromocto, probably forms the only artificial diversion of water, for the facilitation of navigation, on the St. John or its tributaries.

### THE OROMOCTO RIVER.

The Oromocto (Deep River) has two principal branches which, emanating from large lakes about twenty-five miles apart, unite twenty miles above the mouth of the stream, and it flows almost sixty miles from the source of the north branch, and

drains eight hundred and ten square miles. North
Branch Lake, one of the largest lakes in the St.
John system, is nine miles long by two and one
half broad, a low flat country surrounding it, where
the scenery is not very picturesque. Tweedside
settlement extends along the northwestern shore;
elsewhere the forest touches the beach. An attractive spot is the White Sand Cove, a shallow
bay of pure transparent water with a bottom and
beach of clean light-colored sand, where clusters
of wild rosebushes grow just above high-water
mark, a tiny rivulet babbling through them on its
way to the lake. Good fishing may be had, at
times, in the White Sand Cove; for large trout,
while rapidly diminishing in number, still frequent the North Branch Lake. A better place for
small trout is at the southwestern end, where a
deadwater brook enters, navigable for canoes.

All geographers assert that the overflow of the
lake found an exit through this brook, pre-gla-
cially, into the Magaguadavic River, but two miles
distant, and that the Oromocto water to-day is on
a level one hundred and twenty feet above that
river's bed. But how can this be so, when the
north branch of the Oromocto is navigable almost
everywhere for canoes, and reaches tide level at
the forks, after running but twenty-five miles;
while the Magaguadavic, below the supposed
brook outlet, is fifty miles long, with two large
falls on it? There is certainly a discrepancy

somewhere that local geologists will please explain.

From the southern end of Oromocto Lake a portage of three miles leads to Big Kedron Lake on the Magaguadavic. The Jaws Basin, where the north branch emanates, is probably named from its indented coast line; and south of this a wooded peninsula, erroneously called " Kelly's Island," connects with the mainland by a narrow isthmus of sand. The north branch receives the Lyon Stream, the Yoho River, flowing from Lake Erina, Hardwood Creek, and Porcupine Brook. In the bed of the stream a flat rock appears, covered with ancient Indian inscriptions, similar in general character to those so commonly found at Fairy Lake in Nova Scotia.

The south branch of the Oromocto issues from a lake five miles in length, an excellent water for large trout, situated in the rough wilderness of northeastern Charlotte County, near the source of the Lepreaux. It flows in part through an ancient lake basin, where the soil is a fertile alluvium, receiving Sand Brook and Shin and Back creeks, all goodly streams. Canoes may ascend at ordinary water, but with some difficulty, and at least one portage, that around the fall, is necessary.

The northern rivers seem to have a much more constant water supply than those near the Bay of Fundy. Such streams as the Meruimpticook and

Quisibis may be navigated at times when the South Oromocto and Nerepis, draining equal areas, have actually dwindled down to nothing.

The deadwater so characteristic of the Oromocto begins, on the north branch, below the natural fall at Hart's Mill; on the south branch, below Back Creek, and extends uninterruptedly to the mouth. There seems to be something a little uncanny about this river. The water has a peculiar warmth, and, although the current is imperceptible, freezes later than the St. John River, which it so affects that the ice below the mouth of the tributary stream makes an earlier start in spring than the ice above. Instead of the Oromocto rushing along to unite with the St. John, like other tributaries in the flood season, the St. John waters pour up the Oromocto and flood the lowlands until a lake is formed, thirty or forty square miles in area. An amusing story is told of a man, who was "on the limits," being carried away by this forcible up-current while standing on a raft insecurely fastened to the bridge at Oromocto village. "On the limits," in New Brunswick phraseology, seems to imply a condition of involuntary retention within certain prescribed boundaries, secured by the obligation of a bail-bond, and lasting until the *lis pendens* is brought before the proper juridical tribunal, or otherwise disposed of.

When the many-colored autumn leaves are

reflected in the water, and the air is laden with the delicious odor of the newly-mown hay, no more enchanting spot can be found than the Oromocto forks. The banks are alluvial, and lined with bushes, beyond which wide fields extend, studded with graceful elm-trees. The scenery becomes less attractive, however, on descending the stream, and in the wild meadows an air of loneliness and desolation prevails which is positively chilling. Here the Rushagonish, also deep and dead for many miles, enters from the west; the principal tributary of the Oromocto, formed by the junction of two streams that rise in Kingsclear Parish, above Fredericton. The upper waters, as indeed the sources of almost every stream in any way contributing to the Oromocto, abound in small trout, a rather strange fact, considering the habit of that fish to seek the purest and coolest water. It would more accord with the usual custom if all the trout passed up the St. John, and ignored "Deep River" entirely.

Three Tree Creek enters the Oromocto four miles below the forks. The origin of its name is obscure. French Lake, two miles long by one broad, is a pretty little water, surrounded by farm land, and connected with the river by a deep, sluggish channel. The trout which formerly frequented it have become as scarce as ichthyosaurs since the fatal day when pickerel were introduced into the first Eel River lake; indeed,

they decrease everywhere in proportion to the
spread and multiplication of those " fresh-water
sharks." As for the objectionable pickerel, they
rejoice in the slowly moving Oromocto, with its
rank water-grass and lily-pads, and no other tributary so teems with them.

### FROM GAGETOWN TO INDIANTOWN.

Every phenomenon of the St. John, so far considered, has its parallel in some other part of
the world. Fresh-water tides are common to the
Amazon, La Platte, St. Lawrence, and many other
rivers. An alluvial deposit where once there was
an inland lake or sea surrounds the lower Mississippi, and the erosive action of the Grand Falls
resembles that of Niagara ; but between Gagetown
and Indiantown (fifty miles) the St. John possesses certain characteristics not found on any
other river known to man. Most noticeable is
the series of great sinuses or lakes that branch
off eastward, each one almost parallel with the
others. Grand and Washademoak lakes and
Belleisle and Kennebecasis bays are their names,
and they deepen, with the greatest regularity, on
approaching the seacoast. Grand Lake is the
shallowest, Kennebecasis Bay the deepest, and
the average depth of the Belleisle undoubtedly
exceeds that of the Washademoak. We may not
here wade through the depths of geological re-
search to discover the origin of such a strange

formation, but will merely observe that these extraordinary fluvial expansions cross the lines of glaciation with what seems to be an utter disregard of scientific principles.

From Jemseg on the east and Otnabog on the west the lands begin to rise, until rugged hills, ranging from two to seven hundred feet in height, become the common feature of the landscape. Above Gagetown one hundred feet is the almost uniform elevation along the southwestern side of the valley, while the river is bounded easterly by great alluvial flats ; but below Otnabog the scenery partially loses its quiet rural charm, more resembling the mountainous aspect of the Hudson. The islands remain alluvial as far as the Long Reach, when they too change, becoming islands of erosion instead of islands of deposit. The mountainous character of the valley continues to the Bay of Fundy. Here and there a very precipitous bluff crops out on the hillside, but usually the slopes are not too steep for forest growth and cultivation.

At Jemseg the river makes a peculiarly sharp bend, called "No Man's Friend," where vessels must tack laboriously, whether sailing up or down before a favoring breeze, the narrowness of the channel making the manœuvre difficult. At Washademoak the river is several miles wide, and clustered with alluvial islands, of which Upper and Lower Musquash and Long islands are the largest. Lower Musquash is the most irregularly shaped island in the St. John, doubling to inclose a fresh-water lagoon of almost equal area with its land surface ; while Long Island contains, in addition to a lagoon, a shallow, swampy lake. Probably the ancient lake basin formerly occupying the present site of the Maugerville flat contracted below Jemseg, and expanded again at Washade-moak to a width of five or six miles, measured from that river's outlet to the head of Otnabog Lake. Otnabog River, which enters here, is a fairly good trout stream, flowing fifteen or twenty miles, in one part through a rugged, deep ravine.

Behind the steamboat landing, known as " John Vanwart's," a steep hill, five hundred feet high, rises abruptly from the water level, the summit commanding a northward view which many consider the finest obtainable along the St. John River valley. Fannen's Brook enters close by, a small stream flowing from a long and narrow lake, where excellent trout may be caught. Above Belleisle are two small islands, respectively if not respectfully called " Pig " and " Hog," unquestionably for want of better names.

The Long Reach of the St. John, where the river flows in a straight southwesterly course for fifteen miles, is a mere continuation, both geologically and topographically, of the Belleisle valley. High hills uprise on both sides, covered with alternating patches of forest and farm land, while the views, whether from highland or water level, are very extensive and picturesque. At the head of the Reach a long and narrow tongue of inter-vale land extends from the western shore, inclosing an inlet, which is called "Mistake Cove," or, colloquially, "The Mistake," from its tendency to induce strangers to sail in under the impression that they have found a mere channel around an island. Oak Point forms the most prominent projection from the usually regular shore line, below which Little River (at least the sixth tributary of that name below St. Francis) and Jones's Creek enter from the west. Little River rises in Long Lake, a considerable body of water over-looked by a lofty, rugged peak called Blue Mountain. The stream has one fall, perhaps twelve feet high. Below Jones's Creek, the Devil's Back, a prominent ridge, uprises on the west. Next we find the Devil's Brook. A superstitious person might really suppose, on penetrating the interior of this region, that His Satanic Majesty had lent Dame Nature a helping hand in its formation, for there is no rougher country in New Brunswick than the Nerepis Granite Range.

A stream entering South Bay, and flowing from Spruce Lake, an irregular water six miles long, is the last of the St. John's numerous tributaries, and one of the least as well.

The river turns abruptly at the lower end of "The Reach," runs four miles southwestwardly, at a right angle with its former course, passes

Brandy Point, and finally widens to form Grand
Bay. This lake-like expansion is undoubtedly
the broadest part of the St. John; but as the
Kennebecasis branches off to the eastward, one
cannot tell just what proportion of the bay should
be computed in the drainage area of the latter
river. In fact the Bay of Fundy tides often pre-
dominate over both.

## THE DRAINAGE AREA OF THE JEMSEG RIVER.

The overflow of the Grand Lake finds an outlet through the Jemseg, a deep, sluggish channel,
six miles in length, draining at low water an
area of fourteen hundred and seventy square
miles, or more land than any other tributary,
excepting the Aroostook and Tobique. As the
St. John (at high water) covers the lowlands in
many places, Grand Lake and its surrounding
waters then find numerous vents, and it is impossible to estimate the percentage of rainfall carried off by the Jesmeg alone.

Grand Lake, already considered in comparison
with Temiscouata, is twenty-nine miles long, with
an extreme breadth of seven miles at Cumber-
land Bay. The superficial area is said to be one
hundred square miles; the rise and fall of tide,
six inches. All portions are shallow, the greatest
depths rarely exceeding ten fathoms, and for several miles above the Jemseg a channel has been
dredged to facilitate navigation. The shores are

low, thereby detracting somewhat from the beauty of the landscape. Cultivated lands surround the lake on all sides, and the canoeist may find attractive camping grounds at any point or bay, and may purchase farm supplies that would be considered rare luxuries on the more northern tributaries of the St. John. Grand Point, ten miles above the outlet, is the most prominent projection from the northwestern shore; on the south side, Cox, Ellesworth, Fanjoy's, and Robertson's points are all conspicuous, the bays between them having the same general trend as the various branches of the St. John below Gagetown. At Robertson's Point, a favorite place for picnicking, there is a curious stone called Table Rock; and above Grand Point a small lake connects with Grand by a narrow channel named "The Keyhole." Coal Creek, a suitable stream for canoeists, enters the northeastern arm of the lake, often called "The Range."

Salmon River, being much the largest feeder of Grand Lake, may be considered geographically a continuation of the Jemseg. Rising in a level tract of wilderness land, forty miles eastward in a direct line of the mouth of Coal Creek, the stream makes a sweeping bend, known as the Ox Bow, whence a portage but three miles long leads to the headwaters of the Richibucto River. Below Ox Bow the general course is southwesterly. It is a quiet stream, navigable for canoes except in the extreme droughts of summer.  The Lake Stream, a principal tributary on the south side, must also be in some degree navigable, as the Indians formerly " portaged " from it to the north branch of the Canaan River.  Yet larger is the Gaspereaux, which, flowing from Gaspereaux Lake and running about thirty miles in a semicircular course, enters Salmon River from the north.

Newcastle Creek, another feeder of Grand Lake, entering six miles below Salmon Bay, has two principal branches, called the Big and Little forks, both of which rise near Gaspereaux Lake. In places the stream has cut through horizontal rock strata so as to form lofty, precipitous cliffs. Similar cañon-like gorges are found also upon Salmon River, exposing in places thin veins of bituminous coal.

We now pass to the southwestern end of Grand Lake, where, opposite the Jemseg outlet, a deep channel, two miles in length, connects its waters with Maquapit.  Maquapit Lake is connected with French Lake by a similar " thoroughfare " of somewhat greater length, and into French Lake empty Little River, Burpee's Mill Stream, and the Portobello.

The Portobello rises in several little rivulets, which cross the old Richibucto road a few miles from Fredericton, and unite as they pour down the hillside upon the upper portion of that great alluvial flat before spoken of as bounding the St.

John River on the east from Nashwaak to Jemseg. The name Portobello, which probably means
"fine portage," or "easy going," has been given
with great propriety, as the water, winding about
through a soft and easily eroded alluvium bed, is
naturally deep and sluggish all the way to French
Lake, a distance of nearly thirty miles by water
from the Richibucto road. The Portobello is a
veritable "meander," even if the Nictaux and
Cabineau rivers are not. No more tortuous stream
can be found anywhere. The banks are often
thickly wooded; and as New Brunswick possibly
surpasses all other countries in the beauty of its
autumnal foliage, the canoeist should visit the
Portobello in October, when the leaves, almost
meeting overhead, throw dazzling reflections upon
the water. But beware the Portobello in June;
there are mosquitoes there then, in number as the
sands upon the seashore, and words may not be
found infernal enough to describe their depreda-
tions.

Blind Lake, an elongated stagnant pond or
"bogan hole," branching from the Portobello, is
reached by "portaging" one mile from the St.
John River, at a point opposite the middle of
Oromocto Island. The water route thus formed,
through the Portobello, French, Maquapit, and
Grand Lakes, and Jemseg, has been named "the
back way," the ordinary river route being "the
front way," although never so termed. Lunan

Brook, another branch of the Portobello, offers the angler a rough wade and a full fish-basket. Burpee's Mill Stream, which rises near the Pennioc, and falls into French Lake after running fifteen or twenty miles, is also a very good trout stream. The wild country about the sources of these brooks is little known, although quite near Fredericton, and small lakes exist there, as yet unmapped. Moose still frequent the region.

It would be tedious to enumerate all the streams in the St. John system, and throughout New Brunswick, that have received no more distinguishing an appellation than that of "Little River," but the largest, undoubtedly, is the one flowing into French Lake, a stream more or less settled for some distance, and "canoeable" at ordinary water. Bear Brook, a principal tributary, may be reached by wood-road from the Nashwaak valley, and whoever delights to catch very small trout in unheard-of numbers should thrust that portion of his body which contains the collected perceptive organs of sense into the folds of a mosquito netting, and pay the brook a visit.

Maquapit, somewhat larger than French Lake, is seven miles long by two wide, and continued eastward in a small river of the same name. Loder Creek, a deep and sluggish channel, connects it with the St. John, thereby cutting off from the Sheffield flat what is virtually a great alluvial island, larger than any other in the basin of the St. John, thirteen miles in length, with an extreme breadth of four miles. The island may soon become mainland, as the creek, once a common and convenient thoroughfare, is said to be badly obstructed by logs deposited during the floods. The southwestern shores of Maquapit, and of the channel connecting it with Grand Lake, were famous Indian camping grounds in prehistoric times, and the muddy banks contain bits of broken pottery, stone implements curiously marked, and flint arrow-heads, which often lie exposed where the alluvium has been eroded by ice, and the loose material filtered by flood-water.

Duck-shooting over the marsh lands of the Jemseg and Oromocto is a favorite sport, and during a freshet, when French, Maquapit, and Grand Lakes invariably become one great irregular sheet of water, the sportsman may lose his bearings in the excitement of the chase.

## THE WASHADEMOAK.

The Washademoak is second in the series of fluvial fiords having the phenomenal parallelism already noted; and the Canaan River, its geographical continuation, which is separated by a very low watershed from the sources of the Buctouche and Cocagne rivers, rises within fifteen miles of tidewater in the Straits of Northumberland. Not only these lake-like expansions of the St. John, but the valleys of their principal affluents, are invariably parallel to each other.

Canoes may ascend the Washademoak and Canaan to the extreme headwaters, the former being twenty, the latter seventy-two miles long. The Canaan closely resembles Salmon River of Grand Lake in its smooth, swiftly flowing current and freedom from falls and rapids. The country about the upper portion of the Washademoak Lake was settled one hundred years ago, when many northern branches of the St. John were quite unknown to the invading white man; but wilderness land, wide caribou plains, and peatbogs still surround the Upper Canaan, no settlement appearing on the stream for many miles. The moose and caribou hunter may yet enter the forests here with reasonable expectations of success. In average width the lake does not exceed three quarters of a mile, but at Belyea's Cove it is three, and at Lewis's Cove four miles from shore to shore. The Canaan north fork is the principal tributary on the right-hand side, and many large brooks enter from the south, often having picturesque falls where they pour down into the valley. Cole's Island, one of the few inhabited islands on the St. John waters, marks the limit of navigation for steamboats and schooners.

### THE BELLEISLE.

Belleisle Bay, eleven miles in length, reposes in a deep valley, which is, as usual, continued eastward much beyond the head of the bay, and

drained by a small stream, likewise called Belleisle. The valley is thickly settled, and very
fertile, the soil being a dark red loam; and
the beautiful scenery of the bay may be viewed
from the deck of a steamboat that ascends several
times a week. A singular promontory, twenty-five
miles long by six broad, known as the Kingston
Peninsula, extends southwesterly between Belleisle and Kennebecasis bays, and is almost divided
by Kingston Creek, a deep indentation of the
southern shore of the Belleisle. Skaters pass up
this creek on their way from Fredericton to St.
John, to avoid the weak and treacherous ice of
the Grand Bay. Another deep cove is found near
the mouth of the Belleisle, running parallel to the
Long Reach on the St. John, and separated therefrom by a picturesque promontory called Gor-
ham's Bluff, the sides of which are bold and
rocky, the top crowned with woods. The southern terminus of the Kingston Peninsula is called
The Land's End.

The Kennebecasis River, or rather lake and
river, forms another remarkable fiord parallel to
both the Washademoak and Belleisle. It rises
in the parish of Waterford, near the sources of
Pollet River (a stream flowing northerly into the
Petitcodiac) and the Point Wolf, a small river
falling directly into the Bay of Fundy; thence it

makes a sweeping bend northeast, north, and west, and, entering one of the parallel valleys, flows southwesterly to Grand Bay on the St. John. The river and lake drain eight hundred and fifty square miles, and their length combined about equals that of the Washademoak and Canaan, the lake alone being eighteen miles long. The Kennebecasis is "canoeable" everywhere, and usually navigable for boats as well. The principal tributaries are Smith's Creek and Studholm's Mill Stream, flowing southerly; and the South Branch, Trout Creek, and Hammond River, flowing north and east. Smith's Creek winds through a narrow valley at the base of Mount Pisgah, and enters the upper Kennebecasis, more often called Salmon River. Hammond River is fed by numerous rivulets intersecting a rugged and highly picturesque country bordering the northeastern coast of the Bay of Fundy, and above the cultivated land at the mouth it rushes through a narrow, rocky gorge. Henry's Lake, near Quaco, was once famous for trout; but since the construction of the St. Martin's and Upham Railway brought this region within easy access of St. John, the number of anglers has ever increased, the number of fish diminished. The valley of Hammond River is approximately parallel to that of the Kennebecasis. Indeed, all the larger streams hereabout seem unable to run otherwise than parallel to all their neighbors, unless when making cross-cuts from valley to valley.

The largest islands encompassed by any St. John water, excluding the great alluvial deposit cut off from Sheffield flat by Loder Creek, are Long and Darling's islands on the Kennebecasis, both inhabited and traversed by roads. Darling's Island connects with the mainland at low water; but Long Island, which is the most elevated as well as one of the largest St. John River islands, stands well off shore. On the east side a huge precipice, called the Minister's Face, rises almost perpendicularly from the water's edge.

Probably no other tributary is so well settled as the Kennebecasis, and on no other can soils of such fertility be found. Norton and Sussex vales are, with Sheffield and Maugerville, the gardens of New Brunswick, and the chances are that no unopened tracts in the interior will ever equal them. The Intercolonial Railway follows the valley for many miles, passing through Rothesay, Hampton, Sussex, and many other pleasant villages, famous as summer resorts for the citizens of New Brunswick's somewhat foggy metropolis, the city of St. John.

Boar's Head marks the southerly termination of Kennebecasis Bay. Although this steep and rugged cape is but fifty feet in height, the water is computed to be two hundred and twenty feet deep at the base, the greatest depth yet found in any St. John water excepting Lake Temiscouata.

## THE NEREPIS RIVER.

The Nerepis River, entering from the west at the foot of the Long Reach, drains a large country between the valleys of the Oromocto and St. John rivers, and receives ten small affluents. It becomes considerably developed, as Mr. Cooney would say, by a gradual expansion, and by the contributions of a variety of undistinguished rivulets. Marsh lands extend along the lower course (annually flooded by back-water from the St. John), where the channel is tortuous and deep, the current sluggish. At ordinary water canoes may ascend the stream to Fowler's Fall, sixteen miles from the mouth. The bridge crossing the marsh lands above Westfield is the longest over any branch of the St. John, but its architectural beauty is somewhat less conspicuous than its length.

Such brooks as flow westerly into the Nerepis originate in a myriad of little ponds and lakes, occupying the depressions in the Nerepis Granite Range. The country is rough and densely wooded; the lakes perfect gems of natural beauty, often lying in deep, cup-shaped hollows. Granite bowlders of all dimensions often cover the outlets and inlets, and over these thick mosses have grown, so hiding the little rills of water beneath that it is sometimes difficult to trace the direction of their flow. Many of the lakes abound with trout, but a person wishing to angle or explore must shoulder his blanket and provisions, and "rough it" in good earnest.

Near Fowler's Fall the river winds through a deep ravine between the mountains, rounding the bases of precipitous cliffs, which confine the valley for a considerable distance. Douglas Mountain, the Eagle Cliffs, and other rugged hills add great sublimity to the Nerepis scenery.

### THE TIDAL FALL.

Two miles from the Boar's Head the river enters the Narrows, a deep chasm, flanked by lofty mural cliffs, somewhat resembling those on the Lower Saguenay, and formed in rocks of similar age. Below the Narrows there is an expansion, and then another chasm, shorter than the first, which contains within its massive walls the famous tidal cataract, where the fresh waters of the river daily struggle for mastery with the phenomenal tides of the bay. The salt water first rushes in with great velocity until it reaches Grand and Kennebecasis bays, over which it spreads quite evenly, losing both speed and power; then the accumulated mass of fresh and salt water pours out again in a rapid that compares with those above Niagara whirlpool. The speed of the current here has been estimated at twenty-five knots an hour.

If it were not for the great catch-basin above

the Narrows, the full strength of the in-rushing
flood would be felt many miles up the river, to
the damage of intervales and islands. The com-
motion at the fall is due to the presence of ledges
beneath the surface, while in the Narrows the
river is always quiet and navigable, but omi-
nously deep. On the brink of the fall an elevated
rocky island appears, separated from the eastern
shore by a narrow channel, and to many the sight
is more pleasing than that of the Niagara rapids,
the surroundings having a greater diversity and
picturesqueness. The best view is obtained from
the mill on the Fairville side, but the visitor
should also scramble along the cliff between the
suspension bridge and Indiantown.

The depth at the fall, between the mill and
island, varies from eight to twenty-two feet;
while in the small basin below, one hundred and
twenty-six feet is recorded, and, in the larger
basin above, from one hundred and twenty-two
to two hundred and four feet. Opposite Indiantown the river is one hundred and ninety-five feet
deep; and in Grand Bay it continues of great
depth, varying from one hundred and four to one
hundred and sixty feet. The water thus attains
greater depths both above and below the Narrows and fall than in them, a fact favoring the
theory that the river's passage from Grand Bay
to the lower basin is through a mere valley of
erosion, as at Grand Falls, rather than through a

crack or fissure produced by some violent separa-
tion of the rock. The existence of a probable
pre-glacial channel extending from the harbor
to Kennebecasis Bay, by way of the Marsh Creek
and Drury's Cove, is yet more conclusive evidence
in favor of the erosion theory. Professor Hind
says: " The falls at the mouth of the St. John
are not falls in the ordinary acceptation of the
term; they result from the narrow and shallow
outlet through which the tide, which rises with
great rapidity, has to pass. The outlet is not
sufficiently broad or deep to admit the tidal
waters with their rise, hence a fall inwards is
produced during the flow; at the ebb the tide
recedes faster than the outlet of the river can
admit of the escape of the waters accumulated
within the inner basin, hence a fall outwards.
The following are instructions for going through
the falls, which apply, we believe, to no other
' falls ' in the world: The falls are level, or it
is still water, at about three and a half hours on
the flood, and about two and a half on the ebb;
so that they are passable four times in twenty-
four hours, about ten or fifteen minutes at each
time. No other rule can be given, as much
depends on the floods in the river, and the time
of high water or full sea, which is often hastened
by southerly winds. For a few days in the
spring of the year, the height of the water in the
river renders the passage of the falls extremely

difficult." Between the falls and the harbor the river contracts, at low water, within a deep and narrow channel between banks of slimy mud; and thus ignominiously it glides along, black and foam-flaked, to mingle its waters with the bay.

# CHAPTER V.

## VARIOUS FEATURES OF THE ST. JOHN.

### DESCENT OF THE RIVER.

THE authorities vary so much regarding the difference in level between various points on the river, that little reliance can be placed upon their estimates. Mr. Hind, in his " Preliminary Report on the Geology of New Brunswick," says : "The St. John (south branch) rises in the State of Maine (latitude 46° 2″) one hundred and fifteen miles west of the old Meductic Fort, below Woodstock. The head of the south branch is 2,158 feet above the ocean. The source of the southwest branch, where the monument is placed under the Treaty of Washington, on the boundary between Canada and Maine, is 1,808 feet; and the northwest branch (in Canada) comes from an elevation of 2,358 feet. St. John Lake, on the south branch, is 1,075 feet above the ocean ; and where the river first enters the province, at St. Francis, its waters are not more than 606 feet above high tide." The following table shows some estimated river levels between Fredericton and Grand Falls:—

|  | Distance. Miles. | Height in Inches. |
|---|---|---|
| From Fredericton to the confluence of tide below Chapel Bar...................... | 4.47 | 0 |
| Confluence of tide to French Bar........... | 3.15 | 43 |
| French Chapel to Cliff's Bar.............. | 7.52 | 129 |
| Cliff's Bar to the head of Bear Island...... | 5.70 | 0 |
| Bear Island to Nackawick................. | 8.54 | 227 |
| Nackawick to Meductic.................... | 4.68 | 55 |
| Meductic to Eel River.................... | 9.25 | 220 |
| Eel River to Griffith's Island.............. | 9.43 | 168 |
| Griffith's Island to Macmullen's............ | 12.26 } | 144 |
| Macmullen's to Presque Isle............... | 8.08 } | |
| Presque Isle to Rivière du Chute........... | 14.77 | 375 |
| Rivière du Chute to Tobique.............. | 12.71 } | 765 |
| Tobique to Grand Falls................... | 21.12 } | |

|  | Feet. | Inches. |
|---|---|---|
| Height of the basin at the foot of the Grand Falls above the tide at Chapel Bar. | 177 | 3 |
| Perpendicular height of the Grand Falls.... | 74 | 0 |
| Descent through the Gorge............... | 45 | 6 |

" As the distance," says Mr. Hind, " from
Fredericton to Grand Falls is 125½ miles, and
the ascent by the river is stated to be only
177 feet 3 inches, according to the levels taken,
this would give a fall per mile of only one foot
five inches." Then he says : " The levels taken
between Fredericton and the Grand Falls are not
accurate. The summit of the Grand Falls is
really more than 400 (419) feet, ascertained by
leveling from Passamaquoddy Bay ; the descent
between the foot of the Grand Falls and Fredericton 298 feet instead of 177 ; and the fall per
mile two feet four inches, instead of one foot five
inches."

The descent of the St. John between St. Francis and Fish River is said to be 50 feet; between Fish River and Grand Falls, 137 feet; while the St. Francis falls 142 feet from the level of Boundary Lake, and the Allagash 308 feet between Chamberlain Lake and the mouth. The mean elevation of the basin of the St. John in Maine is about 850 feet.

Having wandered so far into the statistical labyrinth, the following table may be added, showing the river's breadth at different places, when measured at low water : —

| | |
|---|---|
| At Fredericton .................................... | ½ mile. |
| " Cliff's Bar..................................... | 700 feet. |
| " Nackawick..................................... | 475 " |
| " Meductic ...................................... | 550 " |
| " Eel River ..................................... | 550 " |
| " Griffith's Island............................... | 730 " |
| " Presque Isle................................... | 569 " |
| " Rivière du Chute.............................. | 420 " |

### NAVIGATION.

The various waters of the St. John, including all lakes over ten miles long, or expansions of navigable streams, are navigable about 2,630 miles by canoe; about 450 miles by steamboats and sailing craft. Steamboats ply regularly on the main river between Indiantown and Fredericton, and on the Jemseg River, Grand and Washademoak lakes, and Belleisle and Kennebecasis bays. At high water a stern-wheeled, flat-bot-

tomed boat ascends the St. John to Woodstock,
and would proceed to Grand Falls if the swift
current did not make the voyage too slow to be
profitable. Above the falls navigation improves
·again, but Edmundston is, for all practical purposes, the uppermost limit of possible locomotion
by steam. The Oromocto is deep enough for
ordinary vessels, but rather too tortuous and
narrow; so are the "thoroughfares" connecting
Grand, Maquapit, and French lakes. Temiscouata Lake is long enough to warrant steamboat service when the surrounding country becomes more
populous, and so deep that vessels drawing twice
as much water as any ever built could safely sail
everywhere. Grand Bay, the Long Reach, and
the great eastern fiords make excellent yachting
courses. Grand Lake is rather shallow in many
places, but steamers and wood boats pass regularly
from the Jemseg to Salmon River. Some dredg-
ing has been necessary on the St. John River
above Oromocto.

One afternoon in 1850 a strange sound alarmed
the good citizens of Fredericton. It proceeded
from the water, and was of such unusual character, so shrill and piercing, that many supposed it to be the war-whoop of a savage foe, or
the snort of some antediluvian monster that had
lain concealed for centuries beneath the river's
mud. Everybody hastened to the water front,
where no more terrible object appeared than the

THE PIROGUE AND THE BIRCH CANOE

little steamboat Madawaska, steaming lazily up the stream. A few valiant citizens carried fire-arms on that occasion. Several steamboats had been placed upon the river prior to 1850, but the Madawaska was the first to carry a whistle; hence the unusual sound and the widespread excitement.

Whether we are on the St. John or any tributary, the canoe is indispensable to complete and satisfactory exploration.

Some of the journeys made with the aid of rapid currents are simply phenomenal. In May, 1887, during that year's remarkable flood, the Messrs. Straton paddled from the lower basin at Grand Falls to Fredericton, a distance conservatively estimated at one hundred and twenty-five miles, in fourteen hours and forty-six minutes, delaying at Woodstock to dispatch a telegram. On several occasions camping parties have covered the sixty-two miles between Allagash Fall and Edmundston in one day; and a lessee of the Tobique, at ordinary water, decamped one morning ten miles above the Nictaux, and next morning, but an hour or two later, grounded his canoe upon the beach at Andover. Several times have Fredericton canoeists, in the freshet season, paddled home from Shogomoc in four and one half hours, a distance of forty-five miles, and instances of fast canoeing over various St. John waters might be multiplied indefinitely. The statement that unwieldy log-rafts leave Tobique at sunrise during high water, and shortly after nightfall reach Springhill, one hundred miles below, without other motive power than the current, would challenge all belief, if the fact of their annually doing so was not well known.

Col. John Allen, in his " Report on the Indian Tribes " written in 1793, says: " The Indians have told me, when the stream was rapid, they have delivered letters to the French commanding officer at the mouth of the St. John in four days from Quebec."

## BRIDGES AND FERRIES.

Eleven bridges span the St. John River, six for roads and five for railways. The steel cantilever bridge of the St. John Bridge Company and the suspension bridge at Fairville, both crossing below the tidal fall, nearly one hundred feet above the water, and the suspension bridge across the Grand Falls gorge, are the most interesting, while the Fredericton bridges are conspicuous for length. The only large tributaries yet unbridged are the Allagash and Little Black rivers.

A peculiar feature of the upper St. John is the number of ferries that are worked solely by the river current. A wire is suspended from bank to bank fifteen or twenty feet above water, and the ferry attached at both ends to a rope, which passes over a little wheel, the latter running along the wire. By regulating the position of the rope, the ends of the ferry are kept at unequal distances from the wire, and in the direction of that end which is least distant the said ferry invariably moves.

Horse ferries are used in a few places, and, until recent years, three steam ferries, peculiarly unique in architectural design, carried passengers, when any offered themselves to be carried, and at other times their captains and engineers, between Fredericton and its trans-riparian suburbs.

### DENUDATION OF THE FOREST.

Although the only affluents of the St. John yet totally surrounded by forest are the south and southwest branches, there is but one settlement in the basin of the northwest branch, and that consists of a few French farms, near small brooks entering La Rivière Noire, a branch of the Daaquam. On Black River the only settlement is St. Pamphile, and Little Black River and the Chemquassabamticook are unsettled above their mouths. A few isolated farms, unconnected by road, contain the only lands on the Allagash and on the St. Francis (between Glazier and Boundary lakes), denuded of natural forest growth. The Great Fish River region is more or less settled from Portage Lake to Fort Kent, although, above Nadeau Lake, the cleared lands never extend to the stream. Above Portage Lake the

forests are intact. The main Meruimpticook has
no settlers above the intervale land at the mouth;
and while the Madawaska River and the western
shores of Temiscouata are well settled, the valleys
of the Touladi, upper Cabineau, and Ashberish
rivers are still invested with luxuriant forest
growth. Green River is unsettled above the east
branch, the Aroostook above Ox Bow, the Tobique
above Nictaux, the Nashwaak above Rocky Brook.
While the valleys of the tributaries below Fredericton are more closely populated, it is very
doubtful if even one of these streams has a drainage basin less than half clad in a dense growth of
trees.

What will happen when all this territory is
deprived of its present sylvan character? The
annual freshets, already somewhat afflictive, will
undoubtedly increase in proportion to the dimin-
ution of woodland. In the Connecticut valley,
where the forests have been largely cut down or
burned, the floods are said to surpass those of the
St. John, while the average rainfall cannot be
much greater, and may be less; and on the Ohio
a difference of sixty feet is recorded between ex-
tremes of high and low water. Such a rise on
the St. John at Fredericton would submerge
everything but church steeples. One obvious
reason why forest denudation is followed by an
increased violence in the floods is that snow, collected in severe winters, lies more exposed to the

sun's rays in spring. It must be remembered however, that forests themselves induce rainfall, according to some coöperation of natural causes not fully understood.

In the St. John valley, where the winters are almost arctic in severity and snows accumulate for many months, many people live on intervale lands, and a satisfactory solution of the various moot questions relating to forest and flood may one day become of vital importance. To illustrate the rate at which the denuding process goes on, I may state that, in the present year, 1893, fifty millions of feet of lumber were cut within the Aroostook valley alone. Forty years ago the Tobique was almost entirely unsettled, and Mr. Cooney described it in 1832 as "a river bathing the unimproved and almost unknown lands of the county of York," but now there is a road to the Nictaux, sixty miles above the mouth, and a succession of prosperous farms. On other tributaries the settler and his axe have advanced almost as rapidly.

### THE FRESHETS.

The highest freshet ever known to occur on the St. John was that of May, 1887, when the water covered a considerable portion of the Fredericton town plot, carried away numerous bridges, and devastated the lowlands of Sheffield and Maugerville for over a week. As usual, the principal water came from the upper St. John, the Aroostook River probably being the largest contributor. So feeble, in comparison, was the stream of the Madawaska, that the St. John, backing up, lifted the Edmundston bridge from its abutments and deposited it on the bank above. The flood assumed phenomenal proportions at Fredericton on the fourth of May, and on the thirteenth of that month a rapid subsidence began. The lower tributaries, especially the Nashwaak, reached their highest level a week sooner than the St. John at Fredericton; as the snow above Grand Falls thaws later, and it takes several days for the water of the more northerly tributaries to reach Fredericton. The little village below the Nashwaak, sometimes called "Tattletown," was in a bad predicament, the water sweeping through it very forcibly, and compelling people to evacuate their shops and interchange visits by boat in a manner quite ultra-Venetian. As the land was lower in the Portobello depression than on the immediate river bank, the current quickened wherever an inlet that way was afforded. In Maugerville and Sheffield many farmers fled with their goods to the highlands, and in a few localities the water is said to have entered second-story windows, and there deposited logs, so that their ends protruded after the subsidence took place. In some of the barns, floating floors were made for cattle, but this novel expedient failed to insure

their safety in at least one instance, where it is
said that a few of the unfortunate animals were
crushed against the stationary floor above. The
flood country presents a somewhat melancholy
aspect when houses, barns, haystacks, and leafless
trees arise above a desolate waste of turbid waters; and in the vividness of his imagination the
spectator is carried back to the coal period, almost expecting to see some huge, misshapen rep-
tile emerge above the labyrinths of sunken bushes.

As the tidal inflow through the Narrows above
Indiantown is distributed evenly over Grand Bay,
spending its force less than twenty miles inland,
so does this wide expansion scatter the flood-water,
which might otherwise rise to a dangerous level,
when checked in its outlet by the narrowness of
the channel. The current at Fredericton was
more rapid during the first stages of the flood of
1887 than afterwards, when Grand Bay and the
other catch-basins were filled, and so vast an
amount of water was backed up that the Nerepis
flats were inundated several days after the subsidence above. The unusual outpouring of fresh
water is said to have prevented the tide from
entering St. John harbor, and by all accounts
"the reversible cataract" became a truly inspiring sight.

Mr. G. F. Matthew, speaking of the remarkable retention of flood-water by the Narrows in an
article "On the Occurrence of Arctic and Western

Plants in Continental Acadia," says : " These pent-up waters are then compelled to spread themselves over the lowlands of the valley of the river and such affluents as the Kennebecasis, Nerepis, Washademoak, Belleisle, Grand Lake, and the Oromocto. Two extensive though very irregularly shaped lakes are thus formed, — the lower one extending, in the form of an oxbow, down the valley of the Kennebecasis, around Grand Bay, and up the " Long Reach " and Belleisle Bay ; the upper one embracing a large area, beginning at the lower end of Long Island, and extending upwards over the lowlands lying around the Washademoak River, Grand, Maquapit, and French lakes, and all the intervale lands between Gagetown and the Oromocto, submerging also the lands on each side of this river for many miles up. The area of these lake-like expansions of the St. John River, which lie partly among the southern hills and partly to the northward of them, cannot fall far short of 600 square miles."

### THE ICE.

Excepting the principal waterfalls and " airholes," and possibly the Madawaska River above Dégelé, ice forms on all waters of the St. John above the Narrows. The " air-holes," which are small open spaces, usually oval-shaped, that rarely or never freeze over, although surrounded by strong, thick ice, often appear in the same places winter after winter, and originate from causes not very well understood. Some are near the mouths of tributaries, others near springs. A changeable winter often forms thicker ice than one of steady cold, as every thaw is followed by a freezing of surface water poured down from the banks.

Experiments recently made at Fredericton have again illustrated the fact that solid ice may move within itself, that is, by an alteration of the relations of its component particles, without any fracture, or general movement of the entire mass. Stakes were placed in a straight line between the banks, and some months later the line of the stakes had assumed a curvature downstream, the distance from the original line increasing with the distance from the river banks.

The average duration of the period when navigation is closed at Fredericton is one hundred and forty-four days. Once within the memory of residents now living, the ice ran out in January, during a midwinter thaw of unusual clemency, but as a rule the river is solidly frozen over from the latter part of November until the middle of April. Even the rough rapids above Allagash are annually coated with ice, said to be sufficiently thick to support a span of horses and heavily loaded sled. At times the river affords unrivaled skating facilities, the part between Fred-

ericton and Gagetown being usually the best.
Skaters occasionally quit Fredericton in the early
morning, and reach Clifton on the Kennebecasis
by nightfall, thus leaving seventy-five miles of
glaciated river marked up with their tracks. As
the Grand Bay ice is seldom safe, because of tidal
fluctuations, the skaters proceed up Kingston
Creek from the Belleisle, and walk to Kennebecasis Bay. From Fredericton to Oromocto, and
more rarely to Gagetown, the river surface is
often one continuous ice-sheet, so smooth that it
vividly reflects the surrounding landscape. The
Oromocto stream is not so safe for skaters, being
warmer water; and the rapid currents above
Fredericton make the ice in that direction rather
treacherous. After the ice has formed, a rise
in the stream often loosens it along the banks,
where flood-water is pressed up, forming, as it
freezes, bands of yellowish colored ice, called
"shore streaks," which usually have a glassy appearance, and are very pleasant to skate upon.

When well frozen, the St. John affords a common highway, and several Fredericton streets are
annually continued across the ice and marked by
lines of spruce bushes. Before the bridges were
built, these "street continuations" often changed
places with a partial movement of the ice, allowing people to walk down Carleton Street, for instance, to the water front, and proceed across the
river on what was but one day, possibly but one

hour, previously a continuation of York Street. The general ice-run, which causes much damage, usually precedes the water-flood by a week or ten days. Wharves and bridges are liable to be mutilated, or completely demolished; alluvial banks eroded, large trees uprooted. In one instance the upper story of a wooden house, built on a jetty on the bank, was swept away *in toto*, the occupants barely escaping with their lives. On the islands and intervales, barns are chained to trees, but not so much for protection against the all-powerful ice as against the subsequent freshet, when real estate sometimes travels with a facility usually accorded to personal property alone.

In years gone by, several bad "ice-jams" have occurred near Fredericton, damming the water to a dangerous height. On the 11th of April, 1831, one of these "jams," at Simond's Point, two miles below the town, inundated all the front streets; and so sudden was the breaking up throughout the river's course, that immense ice-cakes got stranded, or upturned like polar bergs, rising even to the level of the housetops, and threatening the town with destruction. In 1854, or thereabouts, an ice-jam raised the water to a level which certainly equaled, perhaps exceeded, the maximum flood-level in 1887; and cannon were discharged over it, in order that the concussion might loosen the mass. The whole plain was swept by water and ice a short time before the landing of the

Loyalists. At another time numerous congealed
fragments of the St. John and its tributaries
formed an incredibly high dam near Keswick; but
there being no city to submerge above that point,
the accumulated mass was considerately permitted
to disintegrate by natural processes alone. In
April, 1887, another " jam " occurred in the same
locality, which existed several days, while on the
wharves at Gibson ice-blocks were piled thirty or
forty feet high. The rapidly rising water wore
away the Keswick jam, and some of the detached
cakes congealed together, and descended the
stream as bergs, sufficiently large to ground in
deep water opposite Fredericton.

When a severe and snowy winter is followed by
a rapid change in spring, or by heavy rains, the
freshet consequent thereupon tears the strong ice
from its riparian fastenings, causing a violent
"run;" but when the thermal change is slow, or
unattended by heavy rainfall, the ice rots gradually, or melts away without much motion.

Five miles an hour may be considered the maximum speed of running ice below the Keswick
islands, and the display generally commences with
the movement of one huge cake extending from
bank to bank, followed by a procession of smaller
ones. The abutments of the bridges cut them like
knives. Later comes the broken ice, affording a
much more curious spectacle. The blocks are of
all shapes and sizes, jumbled together in one

great mass, from which a grinding, crunching sound proceeds, varied at times by the bellowing of unfortunate cattle contained in some barn that has been picked up and carried away without the slightest resulting liability for trespass or larceny. The ice of this confused mass, having traveled some distance, is discolored by mud and turf torn from the banks. The *tout ensemble* is decidedly imposing.

In the principal lakes the drifting and expansion of ice often cause peculiar dynamical effects. On the southern shore of Grand Lake, below Dykeman's Beach, a ridge of stones and gravel has been formed, perhaps twenty feet in height. Trees cluster on top, and behind the land recedes into a swampy flat. In frosty nights, when the mercury is many degrees below the cipher, the great ice-fields contract so violently that their mass is fractured; and cracks appear, which rapidly extend in all directions, emitting sounds by no means musical. A rapid rise in the temperature creates expansion, the ice becoming pressed up in ridges when unable to overcome the lateral resistances. On Grand Lake these glacial ridges are said to attain a height of ten feet, and they frequently break along their summits, forming curious faults and overlapping strata. It is but a miniature of the great terrestrial change by which the loftiest mountains have been uplifted from the seas, the continents created, the earth made fit for human habitation.

On the lower waters the phenomena of ice and
flood are especially interesting. After the ordinary freshets of the Washademoak, Kennebecasis,
and Nerepis have subsided, the flood-water from
the upper St. John appears and spreads up the
depressions of these rivers, causing a second overflow of greater magnitude than the first. On the
Kennebecasis this second flood is called the " back-
freshet." So the ice of the upper waters is discharged into the Grand Bay two weeks after the
local ice has passed the Narrows, and there it
drifts about (when the winds are southerly), ex-
erting a chilling influence upon the air, and re-
tarding vegetation.

### THE FISHERIES OF THE ST. JOHN.

The subject of the fisheries is too comprehensive
a one to be exhaustively discussed in a work of
the present kind, but the reader is referred to the
reports on the sea and river fisheries of New
Brunswick by the late M. H. Perley, Esq., from
which much of the following information is derived.

Of all fishes found within the waters of the St.
John, the brook trout (*Salmo fontinalis*) is the
one most generally distributed. Nearly every
stream and lake is supplied with a greater or less
number of them, and they vary in weight from
one ounce to five and a half pounds. Says Mr.
Perley : " The brook trout is a migratory fish :

when in its power, it invariably descends to the
sea, and returns to perpetuate its species by de-
positing its spawn in the clearest, coolest, and
most limpid waters it can find. Various causes
have been assigned for the great variety in the
color of the brook trout. One great cause is the
difference of food ; such as live upon fresh-water
shrimps and other crustacea are the brightest;
those which feed upon May flies, and other common aquatic insects, are the next; and those feed-
ing upon worms, the dullest and darkest of all.
The color and brilliancy of the water has also a
very material effect upon *Salmo fontinalis.* The
fish of streams running rapidly over pebbly beds
are superior, both in appearance and quality, to
those of ponds or semi-stagnant brooks."

As illustrating these principles, it may be stated
that trout caught in the clear water of the White
Sand Cove, Great Oromocto Lake, are usually
bright and light-colored, while those found in the
sluggish creek at the southern end of that lake
are very dark. The trout of the Tay and Undenack, clear-water tributaries of the Nashwaak
River, are much brighter than those of the Pennioc and Napadogan, where the water is darker;
and the trout of Green River and the Tobique are
lighter in color than those of Great Fish River
and the Allagash. Mr. William McInnes, of the
Canadian Geological Survey, speaking of the trout
on the west or lake branch of Green River, says:

"They are very noticeably different from those of the main stream, being deeper colored, of great width in proportion to their length, and more sluggish in movement." Nearly all the quiet waters of the river are on the west branch.

The great gray trout (*Salmo ferox*), better known as the "togue" or "touladi," is found in great numbers, and of large size, in the lakes of the Madawaska, Fish, St. Francis, and Allagash rivers, as well as in Lac de l'Est and elsewhere. In Lake Temiscouata the fish has been taken of the weight of twenty-one pounds, and the most sportsman-like way of catching it is by "trolling" from a canoe or boat in early spring. Mr. Perley thus describes the "touladi:" "When in perfect season and full-grown, it is a handsome fish, though the head is too large and long to accord with perfect ideas of symmetry in a trout. The colors are deep purplish brown above, changing into reddish gray, and thence into fine orange yellow on the breast and belly. The flesh is orange yellow, not the rich salmon color of the common trout, when in good condition; the flavor coarse and indifferent. The stomach is very capacious, and generally found gorged with fish; it is very voracious, and well deserves the name of *Salmo ferox*."

The salmon (*Salmo salar*) enters the St. John at the latter part of May, or rather the male fish does; the female appearing a month later, and the grilse, or young salmon, last of all. It seldom "takes the fly" on the main river, but, like the trout, becomes thoroughly sportive on attaining the clear, cold Tobique. The change of water both improves its quality and produces a radical change of habit.

In former years the salmon frequented all the principal southern tributaries of the St. John, more especially the Nashwaak, Oromocto, Canaan, and Kennebecasis, with the two Salmon rivers, where now they are virtually extinct. On the Nashwaak their disappearance is chiefly due to the construction of dams and mills, — for what fish will venture up a stream paved several feet deep with decomposing sawdust? — while on the Kennebecasis and Canaan it has resulted from insufficient protection. Mr. Venning, in a report to the local government, says with regard to the Kennebecasis, "The inhabitants seem to be actuated by an insane desire to destroy every salmon that appears in its waters."

The Tobique, from its swift current, pure cold water, and favorable situation, is preëminently the salmon stream of the St. John system ; and when the fish are prevented by the Grand Falls from ascending the main river, turned away from Salmon River by obstructions in the channel, and disgusted with the Aroostook's impurity, or wearied with unavailing efforts to scale the rapids of its gorge, they seek this noble stream, where all

conditions favor them, and no rapacious pickerel
are found to prey upon their young.

The American yellow perch (*Perca flaves-
cens*), common in the quieter waters of the St.
John, is greenish yellow above, with golden yellow sides, crossed transversely by seven dark
bands, the broadest upon the middle of the body,
and is white beneath. The back and tail fins are
brownish, the others scarlet. "The general hab-
itat of the perch," says Mr. Perley, "is in lakes
and streams not too rapid. It delights in a clear
bottom, with a grassy margin, or in rivers overhung with brush, and widening into some lake-
like expanse. Here the perch roam in shoals, descending and rising while seeking their food, and
shading from the too great heat among the aquatic plants, or under the broad leaves of the water-
lily. The fish spawns in May, then resorting to
the mouths of rivulets in great numbers."

The striped bass, although a salt-water fish,
ascends the fresh-water streams to breed in the
spring, and for a shelter during the winter. In
length it varies from one to three feet, and very
large ones have been taken in the St. John River,
and in Grand Lake, by night lines in the winter
season. It is a good fish for sport, being very
active, and frequently rising to the fly.

The "white perch," so called, is really a small
variety of bass, inhabiting sluggish waters near
aquatic plants and weeds. In weight it varies

from four ounces to a pound, and the flesh, when in season, is very edible. Perch sometimes rise to an artificial fly, but are commonly caught by bottom fishing, with worm bait.

The "pond" or "sunfish," which is not very eatable, being bony and dry, frequents the same waters as the yellow perch. Mr. Perley says it is often caught for amusement, but observation leads one to believe that it is more often taken through an inability to keep it off the hook when fishing for something better, — a variety of sport that is fully as well calculated to tantalize as amuse.

The common sucker, varying in length from ten to fourteen inches, abounds in all the sluggish waters. It is not very good for food, and the least gamey of all the fishes. Another frequenter of sluggish places is the yellow shiner, a delicate, finely flavored fish, much too small for sport. The red-fin, roach dace, and shining dace, or shiner, are three other small fishes often associated with trout. They are good for food (the red-fin especially so), and in the best condition in May.

No fish is more common than the chub (*Leuciscus cephalus*), a coarse fish, sometimes weighing over three pounds. Now and then it takes the fly, to the disgust of the inexperienced angler, who fancies he has hooked a handsome trout. Among the small fishes are the minnows, found in

almost every brook, and useful as bait for larger
fish.

The American smelt, a savory fish, sometimes
taken a foot in length, but generally five or six
inches, is captured in great numbers along the
lower St. John in early spring, before the flood-
waters have subsided. It is named, according to
Mr. Perley, from a peculiar smell, resembling
that of cucumbers. Smelt feed largely on
shrimps, and a piece of any crustaceous animal
will answer for bait.

In the great lakes of the Madawaska, Fish, and
St. Francis rivers we find the whitefish (*Core-
gonus albus*), called the " gizzard fish " by lumbermen, and " poisson pointu " by the French.
The pool below the Little Falls at Edmundston
was once famous for whitefish, the natives taking them with dip-nets in large numbers, but the
erection of the dam proved destructive to this
fishery. In Lake Temiscouata the whitefish
often exceeds three pounds in weight, and is very
delicious, but in the lower waters it seldom exceeds a pound and a half. Mr. Perley thinks
that the fish of this species found in Grand Lake
and the lower St. John were swept over the
Grand Falls, having ventured too far from the
great lakes on the northern tributaries, and he
gives the following description of their habits:
" During the summer, the whitefish is not seen
in Lake Temiscouata, and it is then supposed to

retire to the depths of that unusually deep and cold lake. In October it draws near the shore, and ascends the Tooladie River during the night for the purpose of spawning. Having deposited its spawn, it retires as quickly as possible to the lake. When the fish draws near the shore, prior to spawning, the fishery is carried on, chiefly in a little bay in the lake, where the Tooladie empties. The great gray trout (*Salmo ferox*) follows the whitefish to the shore, and preys upon it. While the nets are set for the whitefish, the fishermen with torch and spear attack and capture the *Salmo ferox*, frequently of large size ; hence the latter fish has acquired the name of 'tooladie,' from the river to which it is attracted by its favorite prey." An early Maine explorer, speaking of the fish in Eagle Lake, Fish River, says: " The kind most sought after is the whitefish. It is the work of but a short time to load a horse."

Shad ascend the St. John to Fredericton, and resort for spawning to Grand Lake, Darling's Lake on the Kennebecasis, Douglas Lake on the Nerepis, Washademoak Lake, Otnabog Lake, and the Oromocto River. They vary in length from one to two feet. The gaspereau ascends the river to the same localities as the shad.

In Lake Temiscouata, and the lakes of the Fish and St. Francis rivers, the fresh-water cusk is not uncommon. The body of the fish is compressed and somewhat eel-shaped, and it hides under stones, waiting and watching for prey. Many are taken near Fredericton, at the beginning of winter, by night lines dropped through the ice, but the best fishing ground is said to be on the sand-bars above Oromocto. The length of the fish varies from eighteen inches to two feet; the weight sometimes exceeds six pounds; and the flesh is white, firm, and of good flavor.

Fresh-water eels are plentiful in all the more sluggish waters. They vary in length from six inches to two feet or more, and may be captured with hook and line or by spearing. Passing by the unsightly catfish (*Pimelodus catus*) as a nuisance to fishermen, we have, for final consideration, the sharp-nosed sturgeon, greatest in size among the fishes of the St. John. The sturgeon formerly ascended the river in considerable numbers in May, and basked upon the shoals above Oromocto and southward of Grand Point in the Grand Lake, but they are now almost extinct in this vicinity, a result of over-fishing. The lamprey eel, fastening upon their bellies and eating into the flesh, caused the big fish to jump high out of the water in their struggles for freedom, and they are said to have fallen on canoes in these unadvised attempts at aerial locomotion. This must have been embarrassing, especially when the fish was full-grown, or from six to nine feet long.

### INSECTS.

We grieve to say that the beautiful forests of the St. John are infested by hordes of mosquitoes, black flies, moose flies, and midges, that lurk beneath the leaves and copsewood until an unsuspecting foe appears, when, less fearful of death than Zulus on the plains of Africa, they shout their battle-cry (at least the mosquitoes do, — black flies are not so civil) and rush to the attack from all sides.

Midges are called "bite-'em-no-see-'ems" by the Indians, and worse names by white men. Certain localities have especially infamous reputations for insects, but a difficulty arises in attempting to localize with accuracy the principal centres of torment. It may be true, speaking generally, that the country above the Grand Falls is worse for black flies than that below; and the country below, more especially that drained by the marshy waters of the Oromocto and Jemseg, a worse mosquito ground than the region above, midges being a luxury quite evenly distributed. June is the worst fly season on the lower waters, but above the falls, where the winters are longer, the insects seldom attain their full numerical strength before July. They bite very assiduously during the earlier weeks of August, but vanish when September comes. Stories might be told of these fiendish little invertebrates that would "harrow up the soul," did the design of this work permit.

The temperature has a marked effect upon insects, as they seldom bite when the mercury is above ninety degrees, or below fifty degrees. About seventy-five degrees Fahrenheit may be considered the favorite biting point. Many concoctions are used to repel their sanguinary onslaughts, but none more efficacious than "slitheroo," a mixture of tar with bear's grease. When this compound is applied in layers of sufficient thickness *les mouches* never bite through it, simply because they cannot.

### THE DISPUTED TERRITORY.

For many years the region drained by the upper St. John and its important affluents, the Allagash, Fish, and Aroostook rivers, was the subject of serious controversies between the governments of the United States and Great Britain. By the treaty of 1783, the northwestern boundary of Nova Scotia (then including New Brunswick) was to be "formed by a line drawn due north from the source of the St. Croix to the highlands which divide those rivers that empty themselves into the river St. Lawrence, from those which fall into the Atlantic Ocean, to the northwesternmost head of the Connecticut River." Unfortunately no such division line could possibly be drawn. The Penobscot, Kennebec, and Androscoggin rivers, falling into the Atlantic, were separated by the highlands referred to in the treaty, not from any rivers falling into the St. Lawrence, but from the St. John and its tributaries, emptying into the Bay of Fundy. Disputes arose, attended with much ill-feeling, and under Jay's treaty, in 1794, a commission was appointed to establish the line. The commissioners surveyed a boundary which ran due north from Monument Brook, the source of the St. Croix; but at Mars Hill, on the Presque Isle stream, the old trouble arose between them, the Americans insisting that the north line should extend to the river Metis in Quebec, the English declaring that Mars Hill was the true northwestern angle of Nova Scotia. Work was abandoned. By the Treaty of Ghent, the king of the Netherlands was chosen to arbitrate; whereupon his Majesty mastered the geography of the Chiputneticook, Apmoojenagamook, and Woolastookpectawaagomic as only such an august personage could, and prescribed a boundary line which extended due north from the St. Croix to the St. John river, followed the "thalweg," or deepest channel, to the St. Francis, and thence proceeded by various courses to the northwestern source of the Connecticut. The American government refused to accept the award, and the matter became once more a fruitful source of strife. In 1839 new commissioners were appointed (Mr. Featherstonhaugh and Lieutenant-Colonel Mudge of the Royal Engineers), but the time allowed was insufficient for a satisfactory survey, and the commissioners' report was rejected; finally the Americans crossed the watershed, erected Fort Fairfield on the Aroostook, and a block-house at Fish River, and proceeded to colonize the country. An agent sent to Madawaska by the government of Maine was seized by the British officials and incarcerated at Fredericton. He had distributed some money among the people, the Americans calling it "surplus money of the United States;" the English, "a bribe to induce the natives to break their allegiance to the crown." The Federal government, anxious for peace, offered Maine 1,000,000 acres of land in Michigan as a compensation for the disputed territory. Maine refused to accept this *quid pro quo*, but issued a proclamation declaring that the country had been invaded by a foreign foe, and ordering the militia to hold themselves in readiness for active service. The Provincial government issued a similar proclamation. In 1842 the two nations were on the very verge of war, and Lord Ashburton was dispatched to America, that it might be forever determined whether Maine was in New Brunswick, or New Brunswick in Maine. On this occasion the American government was represented by Daniel Webster, who remained in office expressly for that purpose, and the boundary agreed upon ran due north from the source of the St. Croix, passed near Mars Hill, touched the St. John River three miles above Grand Falls, followed the thread of the stream to St. Francis, ascended the St. Francis to Boundary Lake, and thence ran southwesterly across the two Black rivers and Lac de l'Est to the southwest branch of the St. John, which stream it followed for thirty-two miles. This line forms the international boundary of to-day, and varies but little from that laid down by William, king of the the Netherlands. The "disputed territory" contains 12,027 square miles. By the Ashburton Treaty the United States obtained 7,015 square miles, England 5,012; by the king's line, England would have obtained 4,119 miles, the United States 7,908.

### IN CONCLUSION.

The principal subjects of discussion relating to the geography of the St. John have now been briefly treated, and the writer regrets that the design and scope of the present work prevent a more minute description of the various interesting regions composing that river system. A book might be written about the Tobique or the Madawaska river alone, that would, without digressing from such matters as are interesting to canoeist and sportsman, contain much more material than this. The extent of the country drained by the St. John has been estimated at twenty-six thousand square

miles, an area much larger than that of the
Province of Nova Scotia, and including certain
portions of Dorchester, Bellechase, Montmagny,
L'Islet, Kamouraska, Temiscouata, and Rimouski
counties in the Province of Quebec; Aroostook,
Somerset, Piscataquis, and Penobscot counties in
the State of Maine; and every county in New
Brunswick except Gloucester; but while it is true
that the river, or some tributary, drains a portion
of each of these counties, it is equally true that
no one county is wholly drained by it.

The two greatest game preserves east of the
Rocky Mountains are the wilderness tracts lying
to the eastward and westward of the middle St.
John.   These tracts are of nearly equal area.
One is bounded southerly by the line of the Canadian Pacific Railway (in Maine), westerly and
northerly by the French settlements in Quebec,
and easterly by settlements bordering the valley
of the St. John; the other is bounded westerly by
the settlements of the St. John, southerly by the
line of the Northern and Western Railway, and
northerly and easterly by the valley of the St.
Lawrence and the Intercolonial Railway.  Both
tracts are covered with a luxuriant forest growth,
traversed by innumerable rivers and brooks, and
dotted with lakes of all sizes.  In the Maine
woods the watercourses are more readily navigable than they are in central New Brunswick;
but New Brunswick has a decided advantage in

natural scenery and in the superior excellence of its trout and salmon streams.

The St. John is greatest among the many watercourses by which the product of the eastern forest is transported to the coast; and as a stately tree expands to form branches, twigs, and leaves, so does this noble river ramify; permeating the wilderness in all directions with its many affluents, its lakes and rivulets.

# CHAPTER VI.

## SETTLEMENT OF THE RIVER VALLEY.[1]

THERE are few places of the same extent in North America which possess a history so varied as that of the valley of the St. John. Aside from its purely local annals and associations, already rich for so new a country, it offers not a little of more general interest.

The history of its colonization presents a curious parallel to the varied movements which have colonized North America as a whole. In the case of both continent and valley, the population has been acquired in a series of waves. First of all, the St. John possesses a tribe of Indians, once owners throughout it all, but now forced to a few grudgingly granted plots, and viewed as aliens, if not as inferior beings. It has, secondly, an old and very purely foreign element in the Acadian French, these likewise now crowded to a corner of the goodly extent over which they were once recognized as rulers. Thirdly, it has a pre-Revolutionary New England settlement, a product of

[1] These notes upon the settlement of the valley of the St. John have been furnished upon our request by a local historian.

the same adventuring spirit which sent their kindred colonizing to the westward. To these follow a
few Englishmen direct from the home land. Next
come the Loyalists, a great number, New Brunswick's priceless accession, her Pilgrim Fathers,
her real foundation. Their coming was one result of the Revolution, which thus so completely
changed the course of events for New Brunswick
as well as for the continent. Finally, the valley
contains settlements of the best classes of later
European immigrants, — English, Irish, Scotch,
Danish, and others, who have come to the Province as their kindred have come to the States in
the present century.

The Indians of the valley form the Maliseet
tribe, of Algonquin stock. They are closely akin
to the Passamaquoddies and Penobscots to the
west, and distantly related to the Micmacs of the
north and east. They are much mixed with white
blood, but are upon the whole superior to the majority of the Indian tribes. They possess a fair
physique, and are generally honest and peaceable.
They live by hunting, acting as guides and supple-
mentary woods trades, but make very poor farmers and laborers. At present they are increasing slowly in numbers, a fact which their dilution
with white blood goes far to explain. They were
friendly to the first explorers, and, except for
minor local hostilities, generally stirred up by
one white race against another, they have been so

to the white inhabitants of the valley ever since. Their most conspicuous appearance in history has been in connection with their raids, in alliance with and under command of the French, upon the New England settlements. They have played but a small part in the history of the valley, and have produced practically no effect at all upon the formation of the New Brunswick people. The principal Maliseet villages are upon reservations (1) at Apohoqui, (2) opposite Fredericton, (3) at French Village, a few miles above Fredericton, (4) at Woodstock, (5) at Tobique, (6) at Madawaska, with smaller and more or less temporary encampments near St. John, at Gagetown and other places.

Before the coming of Europeans, there is reason to believe, these Maliseets occupied the river only from Fredericton upwards, the lower part to the mouth being in the hands of the Micmacs. Their principal settlements were upon sites now abandoned, at Méductic, a few miles above Eel River; and at Auk-pahk, now Spring Hill, five miles above Fredericton. Their place-names along the river have happily largely persisted, the names of nearly every one of its branches being of Indian origin.

The authentic history of the valley begins with its discovery by Samuel de Champlain, on St. John's Day, 1604. It was partially explored by one of his lieutenants, and more thoroughly a few

years later by fishermen and fur-traders. About
1635, Charles de la Tour, under authority of a
grant from the king of France, built a strong
fort at the mouth of the river, upon which, and
the great fur-trade it controlled, his neighbor
D'Aulnay Charnisay, of Port Royal (now Anna-
polis) cast envious eyes. The various efforts of
these two men for supremacy in Acadia culmi-
nated in 1645 in the success of Charnisay, who
during the absence of his rival captured and destroyed his fort. The story of the defense of this
fort is the most picturesque in the history of the
St. John, and a great favorite with the local
chroniclers.

Towards the end of the century, large tracts of
land along the river were granted by the French
government to various of its favorites as seign-
euries. The seigneurs were, by conditions of the
grants, to bring settlers, clear land, make roads,
etc., but these improvements were rarely or never
made. Some of the seigneurs lived a half-savage
life with the Indians along the river, but their
rights gradually lapsed, and they were in time
replaced by a few French squatters from Port
Royal (descendants of settlers brought earlier in
the century from France), who settled at St. John
and a few other points along the river.

About 1690, a strong fort was built by Villebon, the French governor, at the mouth of the
Nashwaak, opposite Fredericton. From this fort

went forth the expedition under Villebon and
Villien, which, with the aid of the Indians, carried
such devastation to the New England settlements.
It was here that no less an ambitious plan than
the capture of Boston itself was debated, and some
attempt made to carry it out. To avenge the mur-
derous attacks of the Indians inspired by the
French, in 1696, an expedition from New England attempted to capture Fort Nashwaak, but
was repulsed with loss.

The few settlers on the river continued to increase very slowly in numbers until 1755, in
which year the British government found it necessary to remove the French from Acadia on
account of their continued hostility to the British.
This expulsion presents us with one of the most
pathetic incidents of any history, and one which
has been fully utilized in Longfellow's " Evan-
geline." The settlers on the St. John were not
captured, but fled up the river, and, joined by
other fugitives, attempted to reëstablish themselves in various sheltered creeks and lakes, and
at Gagetown, Fredericton, and other places. But
from these they were driven, and only secured a
friendly resting-place after the arrival of the
Loyalists. Passing far above these new-comers,
they settled below the mouth of the Madawaska.
Lands were soon after granted to them, and since
that time they have spread sparingly up the river,
but rapidly down on both banks, almost exclud-

ing other settlers, to Grand Falls. The most important event of their subsequent history was the transference of nearly half of them to the United States by the Ashburton Treaty in 1842. They are honest and hospitable, but clannish and unprogressive, and show many characteristics of great interest to the student of peoples.

The close of the "French War," in 1759-60, was followed rather by a spirit of restlessness than by quiet in New England, and this manifested itself in emigration. Many thousands of the New Englanders came to Nova Scotia in 1762-64, and a few hundreds of them to the valley of the St. John. They had their choice of almost the entire river, and settled upon the rich intervales of Maugerville, upon the navigable part below Fredericton. At the breaking out of the Revolution they showed sympathy, very natural under the circumstances, with their kinsmen in the States, but this sympathy they very soon transferred to the British cause, and have since been among the most loyal of British subjects. Possessing the sterling qualities of the New Englanders, they made good settlers, and have given to the Province some of her best men. Their descendants still live at Maugerville, probably as unmixed a pre-Revolutionary colony as exists.

The Englishmen who came during the next twenty years were very few in number, and never formed any settlement, but scattered to various points. Their descendants are still to be found at Oromocto and others of the older villages.

In 1783, there came to New Brunswick many thousands of Loyalists. They included those who, either from duty, from conviction, for gain, or various other incidental motives, took the side of the crown in the Revolution. At its close many of them, for active participation, were officially banished from the new States; a few were unwilling to remain under the new conditions; while the remainder, a great majority, were so obnoxious to their successful neighbors that they were forced to leave the country to insure their personal safety. To these Loyalists was granted the site of the city of St. John, and as much of the main river and its branches as was necessary to supply them all with land for settlement. This required the unoccupied lands along the main river as far up as Woodstock, and the accessible parts of the Kennebecasis, Belleisle, Washademoak, and Grand Lake, and in these places accordingly are their descendants to be found to this day. The Loyalists included some of the ablest men of the Colonies, and their descendants form the largest and best part of the population of the St. John valley. In the places, outside of the cities, where they settled, they have received but little addition from immigration, and consequently are very nearly, in some places entirely, of the original stock. In city and country they are advanced and progressive, and show generally the best qualities of the Anglo-Saxon race.

During the early years of their settlement there was some restlessness among the Loyalists, some friction with the New Englanders, and these together with other minor causes sent settlers from both parties to make homes higher up the river. Gradually the river banks above Woodstock, up to Grand Falls, were thus thinly colonized. Early in this century other settlers began to arrive. A disbanded West India regiment settled above the Tobique; Scotch and Irish settlers were brought by the New Brunswick government, or by immigration and land companies, and, the river bank being occupied, were assigned the lands back of it, or tracts above the earlier settlers on the various lower branches. These, together with settlers from the older settlements, extended gradually up the Tobique and other upper branches, and passed above the French on the main river. The people of Maine extended into the Aroostook and Fish River valleys; and so in this century there has been no new wave of immigration, but a slow growth by expansion within and addition from without.

In rapid summary, then, the order of inhabitants in ascending the river is as follows: At its mouth is the Loyalist city, St. John. Then, upon all of the lower river and its great branches, as far as Maugerville, are settled the descendants of the Loyalists, commingled with a few New Englanders and Englishmen and some later immigrants, and a few Indians at Apohoqui. At Maugerville are the New Englanders, above which occur Loyalists again to Fredericton, itself another city of this people. Hence to Woodstock, excepting a few Indians at each place and at French Village, the people are still principally Loyalist. Beyond Woodstock, excepting the Indians at Tobique, they are commingled New England, Loyalist, and later immigrants, the latter especially back from the river, as far as Grand Falls. Thence upwards, as far as Madawaska, the French occur almost exclusively; but beyond Madawaska they become fewer, and are replaced by settlers of various origin to the St. Francis, above which they almost cease. At Seven Islands the last isolated family is passed, and the river remains a wilderness to its extreme source.

CHRISTMAS MAP
OF
THE UPPER ST. JOHN

www.ingramcontent.com/pod-product-compliance
Lightning Source LLC
Chambersburg PA
CBHW030843270326
41928CB00007B/1188